12 Bowie Albums In 12 Months

Dave Ross

ISBN: 978-1-6781-3896-7

Imprint: Lulu.com

Cover artwork by Mark Reynolds

Acknowledgements

My name is Dave Ross. I only exist online under my pseudonym Dave Amitri (also my fantasy tribute band name) and have done since 2008. I write about music for a hobby. I have decided to step out of the shadows for this book and face the world as me. You can find me, mainly on The Afterword and Twitter @DaveAmitri This book, my first, would not have been possible without the help of the following people.

Thanks to all at The Afterword Forum which gave me a platform. The Afterworders who gave me a sounding board, engagement and inspiration to keep going for 12 months. https://theafterword.co.uk/

Thanks to the Twitter account @memorialdevice that inspired this project and has supported it throughout.

Thanks to Merric Davidson at Toppermost for his guidance, advice and support. https://www.toppermost.co.uk/ Twitter @AgeingRaver

Cover illustration by Mark Reynolds. Find him on Twitter Stuff_By_Mark @The_Ren1981

Finally of course thank you to David Bowie himself.

Introduction

Twitter

@memorialdevice

8th January 2021

And we've said it before but on this day we will repeat it. The run of 12, TWELVE, albums from The man who sold the world to Scary monsters is the greatest in history. Nobody even gets close.

And that was the tweet that started it all. I'm a music fan, very much of that glorious period between the late seventies and the mid eighties that spawned post punk, new romantics, electronica and pop. Later on, my tastes shifted as my life changed from young lad about town to marriage, children and "the grind". I'm in my fifties now. Looking back at the music I loved and writing about it has become a hobby I really enjoy. I've been fortunate to discover The Afterword, a forum covering all aspects of popular culture, that gives me a platform and opportunity for feedback that has really helped my development as a writer. These reviews would not have happened without the contributions and comments from the other Afterworders and I've included some of their comments which I feel really add to the experience.

Back to that tweet. As soon as I saw it, it dawned on me that I had never listened to a David Bowie album before. I knew all the hits but his music had largely passed me by. Unforgivable considering how so many of my favourite artists cited Bowie as a huge influence. So, 12 Bowie Albums in 12 Months was born.

A year long project for 2021, deep diving into the works of one of the biggest and most influential artists in popular music and you could say popular culture of the 20th century.

I realised early on that there are millions of words from all sorts of experts already available on the music, lyrics, collaborators, life and times of David Bowie. What I could bring though was a new perspective, looking for where Bowie had found influence and where he had influenced others. I could look back at these albums with nearly 50 years of music to compare it to, much of it influenced by Bowie, without any preconceptions. If you're looking for expert analysis this may not be for you. However, if you're new to Bowie and want to know what to expect, or if you're a huge Bowie fan looking to reignite your fascination for his music, then I hope somewhere in these 12 reviews you'll find a spark of something that either makes you want to listen to these remarkable albums for the first time or the hundredth. I've resisted the temptation to rewrite or tamper with these reviews in any way even if they contain any errors or embarrassments. These reviews are not meant to be definitive, just conversation starters. They are written from the heart with care, consideration and no deliberate controversy intended. I listened to each album at least ten times and wrote about what I heard and felt as honestly as I could.

Month 1

January 23rd

The Man Who Sold The World

For those who aren't aware I am a pop loving 55 year old music civilian who before this project had never listened to a David Bowie album despite knowing all the radio playlist Bowie tunes by heart. I've decided to listen to a Bowie album a month during 2021 from *The Man Who Sold The World* to *Scary Monsters* after being told they are the best run of 12 albums ever. My angle is to try and find where I have heard his influence in the music of my heroes and report it, as so many of them have cited Bowie as an inspiration. Maybe some will become favourites of mine.

Starting my Bowie odyssey with *The Man Who Sold The World* an album made 50 years ago I wasn't sure what to expect. Bowie the great originator at the beginning of a run of 12 great albums. My expectations were high. So I pressed play.

The Width of A Circle began and straight away I heard that guitar swoosh intro straight from Foxy Lady. Now this is no bad thing. I love The Jimi Hendrix Experience but it set the tone for me from the outset. The first few listens became an exercise in spotting Hendrix's influence. At times it could have been Mitchell and Redding providing the backing to Bowie's interesting vocals. This is still no bad thing. Why wouldn't a 23-year-old who was an aspiring musician during the extraordinary Hendrix peak years take influence from him? It got my interest and was the hook I needed to really listen.

That said, I also need to get this out in the open. I heard something else in there, something I hadn't heard for years. I racked my brains and eventually it came to me *Jesus Christ Superstar*. A quick Google showed that the rock opera was made at around the same time as *The Man Who Sold The World* so it sort of made sense but was equally astonishing to think that Lloyd Webber and Bowie were the sounds I was comparing.

Anyway, early observations out of the way, back to The Width of a Circle an 8-minute epic that felt like it could have been used as background music for one of those scenes in *The History Man* that you didn't want to watch with your mum in the room. Then it becomes a regular pub rock chug along while Bowie wails the lyric and wooahs to a close. Dramatic, sensual with rock overtones. A really good start.

All The Madmen starts and I pick up something in Bowie's vocal that makes me chuckle. He sounds a bit like The Monkees Davey Jones, which is all kinds of weird. The song to be honest never really gets going. It just feels a bit flat. Then at the end I got some Bowie familiarity in the hand clap, repetition, fade out. Next!

I really like **Black Country Rock. It'**s another Hendrix Experience vibe. Bowie's vocal is great and the guitar riffs and the fantastic rhythm section keep the whole thing going. I got a whiff of The Cult and there's a vocal part that Marc Bolan clearly enjoyed and ran with. A highlight for me.

Sorry if I'm committing some kind of sacrilege with **After All** but it's just so dull. I really don't have much else to say about it and I've tried.

I'm bit nonplussed by **Running Gun Blues**. It sounds like the sort of Bowie sound that I recognise but it doesn't seem to go anywhere. My enthusiasm for this project is being tested. I'm beginning to suspect that it's very much of it's time and you probably had to be there. But I'm not a quitter.

Saviour Machine has a guitar sound that would have been at home on Ocean Colour Scene's *Moseley Shoals*. I suspect Steve Craddock had Saviour Machine firmly in mind when he wrote The Riverboat Song. Saviour Machine has an edge and a rhythm missing elsewhere. I can imagine hearing this is in 1971 and really sitting up and taking notice. It's a great song.

She Shook Me Cold is another Hendrix influenced song that you can imagine having a freak out to in a muddy field somewhere stoned, naked and sweaty. I think it's my favourite vocal performance. It's gritty, sexual and probably not for the "Me Too" generation but times have changed.

Now the title track, **The Man Who Sold The World**, the only song I'd heard before listening to the album but possibly only the Lulu version (I know) It sounds like a Bowie song but again, for me, it plods a bit and doesn't really grab me. It's more The Man Who Bored The World.

Maybe we'll finish on a high. **Superman** has Bowie doing his best attempt at a narrative as opposed to singing. It's this song that really brings to mind *Jesus Christ Superstar*, the way the words are almost spoken over a backing track in a "stagey" way. I don't know, maybe this was the way of things in the early 70s. A flat uninspiring finish despite hints of Whole Lotta Love guitar.

In conclusion, this may not have been the best Bowie album for a pop loving hook monster like me to start with. Basically a rock album with no hits and few hooks. It's not immediately accessible and I've listened well into double figures now in the hope the penny drops. I can appreciate the invention but sometimes it felt this was in the place of a tune. (Now I sound like my Dad.) It felt to me like Bowie was trying to find a style and sound and perhaps didn't believe this was it. Knowing the hits like I do, it feels a long way from the sound many radio listening "Oh yes, I love Bowie" types recognise. I've done limited reading on the album as I didn't want to pre-empt my view, but what I have read points me to believe he was being influenced by Tony Visconti and the past rather than influencing the future. Bowie experts will no doubt tell me otherwise. Apparently, they were trying to make an album Cream may have made. I don't know enough about Cream to comment but maybe that's why I didn't find much in there that I recognised in the 80s sound I love by artists inspired by Bowie. I may well return to *The Man Who Sold The World* but not often. This hasn't dulled my enthusiasm as a couple of songs hit the right spot and I'm sure as Bowie finds his way there'll be more for me to enjoy. On to *Hunky Dory* next.

Comments From The Afterword

Arthur Cowslip says

23/01/2021 at 10:00

Wonderful! I am looking forward to your year of Bowie reviews.

I'm not a fan of this album really. It won't surprise you to know he has done a lot better. It's really interesting to hear it from the perspective of someone who is new to this and hasn't heard where he goes next. Like most people who were too young to hear this at the time, I went BACK to this one after being inducted to Bowie by the later albums. And from that perspective, my perspective, what you hear as earnest Hendrix/hard rock influences, I hear as a bit more ironic and theatrical – Bowie "playing" with hard rock and then discarding that mask to go on to other things. But as I say, that's from hindsight, so maybe you are correct and he genuinely wanted to be a rock god at this time.

And YES the Jesus Christ Superstar connection is very apt. I don't think enough of a deal is made of this kind of influence when people talk about Bowie. Wait until you get to Diamond Dogs, where at times you really could be listening to an Andrew Lloyd Webber rock musical, and also bits of Ziggy Stardust, and the song Station to Station. I suppose this might tie into Bowie's theatricality, and his methodical approach to songwriting. There's definitely a very thin wedge between early seventies Bowie and stuff like Evita, Hair and Godspell, etc.

retropath2 says

23/01/2021 at 10:30

"one of those scenes in "The History Man" that you didn't want to watch with your mum in the room", the killer line in a wonderful piece that has me wanting to dig it out and listen, to absorb the love for the influences you are liking less

MC Escher says

23/01/2021 at 13:17

Bowie was desperate to be a star by this point in his career. He'd been around for a good few years, and he must have thought his time was nearly up. So for me this is Bowie doing whatever he could to break big, and he leaned heavily into the Cream/Hendrix style. As such he's following rather than innovating, and fair enough, do what you think will sell. A very patchy record and one I rarely listen to.

Twang says

23/01/2021 at 17:13

Agreed. To be honest he was always a bit of a magpie. I never bought the great innovator thing but he was a genius at repackaging stuff in Bowie style.

For more comments or to join the conversation go to *https://theafterword.co.uk/12-bowie-albums-in-12-months/*

Month 2

February 21st

Hunky Dory

My second dive into 12 Bowie albums in 2021 as someone who had never heard a Bowie album before now brings me to *Hunky Dory*.

February introduced me to 1971's *Hunky Dory*. It's an album that I've seen referenced many times and recommended as one of the great Bowie albums so it was with real relish and anticipation that I dived in. Another brilliantly androgynous cover by the way. I'm looking at you Boy George. A quick look at the track listing and suddenly I had flashes of recognition. Three tunes leapt out as "hits". The ones that radio listening Bowie fans would instantly recognise. I did a little bit of reading but I didn't want to influence my view too much. A first listen and it is a hugely different album to *The Man Who Sold The World* with a huge reliance on piano and less of a rock album. It felt quite messy, eclectic with no definitive sound but in amongst the mess I was able to see that this was a seismic shift towards the Bowie sound. Whatever that is. And it has hits, massive, wonderful hits.

Changes is up first. I have some Proustian emotions from this song. Do I really remember the 6-year-old me hearing this on a crackly radio in my dad's car? I think I do. I had older Radio 1 loving sisters who were more David Essex than David Bowie but something is there deep in my subconscious that I find comforting in this song. Anyway, back in the room how does one avoid clichés when assessing Changes? I'm sorry to tell you I don't. Of course this is a huge change from the previous album. Melodic, soaring and emotive. I suspect Bowie was making a statement. It's an incredible song. One I imagine Paul Weller, never one to hide his influences, leant heavily on when writing Changing Man. There's a similar feel to my cloth ears anyway. A great start for a hit lover like me.

Oh! You Pretty Things next, another hit I recognise and really like. It's definitely a Bowie tune leaning heavily on piano. Piano I instantly recognise as from Elton John's eponymous album, more on that later. Then there's some piano that has a Bohemian Rhapsody drama to it which leads into a sound similar to a school teacher pounding a piano in the school hall. There's even some Hey Jude piano to throw into the mix. The verses are delivered as if in a musical drama by a leading man. Echoes here of The Man Who Sold the World. The chorus however is exquisite. Bowie finds the perfect tone for the delivery of those perfect lines. This is another fabulous song. Inventive, creative, like a Michelin starred recipe combining all those flavours to make an incredible dish. It is such a pretty thing.

Eight Line Poem is a bit of an imposter considering what comes next. Sandwiched between two colossuses it manages to hold its own despite starting with some Claptonesque guitar. It all feels slightly off tune with more Elton piano. I can't pretend to be a Radiohead fan but it sounds like something they might do. Excitingly for me this is possibly the first time I can here Bowie's influence on Billy Mackenzie. This is a song I can hear Billy covering. It would fit very nicely on *Transmission Impossible*. It's a grower and quite lovely.

Life on Mars is up next and whatever I say next will not do it justice but I will do my best. It feels like the song has been everywhere this month as Perseverance made its final descent onto the surface of Mars. The piano intro under Bowie's vocal is straight from Elton's First Episode at Hienton. Which I promise is a huge compliment. I adore early Elton John and I think Elton John remains his best album. I can't listen to Hunky Dory without thinking it was an influence to someone on Bowie's team. It was a stroke of genius if I'm right because it adds a lusciousness to Bowie's edge that is glorious. It's an incredible song. One I've criminally overlooked over the years. If he betters this then I have lots to look forward to. Finally, if Jeff Lynne didn't base ELO entirely on that luscious string outro then I'll see him in court for his defence.

Kooks next. Follow that! Luckily for me it strikes an immediate chord. My boys' music era was the noughties. An indie landfill wasteland to some. To my boys as important as any era, as is the way of these things. Because of this I am aware of the band The Kooks. They were indeed indie and part of the whole Brit school movement. I suspect they were set a project to build a sound from a song and they went the whole hog and went for name and sound. It is uncanny. They built a career on this song yet it doesn't appear to be referenced anywhere. Give them a listen, it's astonishing. The song is OK. It feels a bit lazy after what went before but I don't know how you follow Life On Mars.

Quicksand is a beautiful lament which moves the album on to its second phase. It's another instantly recognisable Bowie song even though I hadn't heard it before this project. I love its easy flow and swimmy feel. I can hear its influence in The Blow Monkeys *Animal Magic*, Dr Robert's vocal delivery and the string arrangements. It's the sort of song I was hoping to discover.

Fill Your Heart is a strange little song. It's more stage musical that wouldn't be out of place on Gilbert O'Sullivan's *Himself*. I'm also instantly put in mind of The Monkees Davey Jones again in Bowie's vocal. I don't know why it's here. Anyone?

Andy Warhol now. My brief reading telling me that this is the first of a trilogy of tribute songs. It makes perfect sense that Bowie would want to create a tribute to Warhol. I'm sure he saw himself in the unique, slightly eccentric, visionary artist. What doesn't make sense is using some chanting rhythms that wouldn't be out of place on an Adam and the Ants song over a Spanish guitar, flamenco hand clap. An odd song that to me is more Picasso surrealism than Warhol pop art.

Song For Bob Dylan is tribute number two. Strangely again it starts with 80s Clapton guitar and becomes straight up mimicry of Dylan unless I'm missing something. I'm not sure about the song and less sure how fans of Bowie would feel if their hero was given this treatment by one of his contemporaries. Maybe Dylan loved it. Maybe you do too.

Queen Bitch is a tribute to The Velvet Underground apparently. A band I admit I know nothing about. It's a great upbeat slice of rock. Post punk new wave guitar and vocal eight years before it was invented. It has driven me mad. I cannot find nor remember the song from that era that has lifted the riff from Queen Bitch. Maybe The Buzzcocks mixed with Mink Deville's Spanish Stroll. If someone could help? Brandon Flowers has admitted to it being an influence on Mr Brightside which is clear in the lyric and delivery. My clear favourite of the tribute trilogy.

The Bewlay Brothers closes and it just sounds like a Bowie song should sound to me. Hints of Space Oddity otherworldly vocals, lyrics left open to interpretation and more than a hint of mystery. I'd imagine Bowie fanboys spending many happy hours picking it apart. Brett Anderson on the other hand made a career out of it. Fair play to him, there is much about Suede to love. It's a great finish to the album for me.

In conclusion *Hunky Dory* reaches astonishing highs and I'm looking forward to listening to it again away from this over-analysis. Unlike *The Man Who Sold The World* I will return to this often. I stick with the view that it's quite messy and by that I mean it doesn't flow and is a mix of styles that don't necessarily fit together as a whole piece. I assume Bowie was still searching. I hope that overtime I see it how others do.

There is so much written about Bowie and this album that I don't expect to have found anything especially new. But my view as an outsider looking in might offer a different perspective. This is the album where I think I've started to "get" Bowie. I'm excited for what comes next.

Comments from The Afterword

Rigid Digit says

21/02/2021 at 19:54

The riff to Queen Bitch.

How about Velvet Underground's Sweet Jane mixed with Eddie Cochran's Three Steps To Heaven

Black Type says

21/02/2021 at 20:57

Re. the Elton (Tumbleweed, ha!) connection. The single Space Oddity was produced by Gus Dudgeon with help from Paul Buckmaster, both heavily involved in Elt's early 70s recordings. And Ken Scott moved from Abbey Road to Trident Studios at the urging of Reg 'n' Gus, when he was still heavily involved in working on their albums. All very incestuous and cross-pollinated...if not vain, and many other last names.

Sorry Dave, pushing ahead of the dames there... Very interesting analysis, btw.

Timbar says

22/02/2021 at 11:13

More than the cross pollination, was the fact that they both were both recorded at Trident Studios, using the same, very distinctive piano.

Ken Scott replied to a query on a Steve Hoffman thread:

"It was a Bechstein grand that, according to Recording The Beatles, was built in 1898. It had a tremendously bright sound that unfortunately was lost when the sound board had to be replaced. Because of it's inherent sound it was remarkably easy to record. Two, maybe three, microphones and just a little eq.

The discography for the piano is astounding.

Bowie – Space Oddity to Aladdin Sane

Elton – Elton John to Madman

Beatles – Hey Jude

Queen, Supertramp, Carly Simon, Genesis, Harry Nilsson and so on.

have heard many pianos in my time but I have never heard a better "rock" piano than that one."

Dave Amitri (aka Dave Ross) says

22/02/2021 at 11:27

Wow. That answers that then. It's remarkable that it wasn't just a sound I recognised it was the same bloody piano!

Tiggerlion says

21/02/2021 at 22:31

Great work! I think you are pretty much spot on.

You can see/hear why Bowie loved Fill Your Heart so much. It's full of goodness, kindness and love. Just forget your head and you're free! He has a lot of fun singing it and it gets the second biggest production on the album (after Life On Mars?). Rick Wakeman's solo in the middle is beautiful.

All the songs on side two are tributes, the first being to Biff Rose and the last to his brother

Lunaman says

23/02/2021 at 14:00

Well done Dave. I'm a lifelong Bowie fan and it's great to hear your appraisals. I saw Bowie play The Bewley Brothers at Hammersmith Odeon 2002. I don't think he had played it live before and it was bliss a magical moment.

I look forward to reading your reviews in future.

For More comments or to join the conversation go to https://theafterword.co.uk/12-bowie-albums-in-12-months-hunky-dory/

Month 3

March 21st

The Rise and Fall of Ziggy Stardust and The Spiders From Mars

Month three into 12 Bowie albums in 12 months as someone who had never heard a Bowie album before and I've arrived at *The Rise and Fall of Ziggy Stardust and the Spiders from Mars*. It will be plain old *Ziggy Stardust* from now on. I definitely approached this with trepidation as it's clearly very important to an awful lot of people. I hope my attempts to view it from a different angle are appreciated. As usual I limited my reading to a scan of Wikipedia and it immediately strikes me how ground breaking the image must have been in 1972. *The Top Of the Pops* Starman performance was obviously a turning point in Bowie's career. I remember how people reacted to Boy George ten years later so in 1972 the concept of a bisexual alien on the telly on a Thursday night must have caused quite a stir. Much Blue Nun spat out into the fondue across 70s suburbia. My mission is to see if the music lived up to the image or was it all flares and no knickers?

On the first listen they'd obviously given Elton his piano back. It's more of a rock album but with some surprising elements that fired up some strange musical and vocal connections and influences for me. Obviously, the whole glam rock movement was spawned from the seed of Ziggy's loins but I also found familiarity across five decades from the 60s through to the early 2000s.

Five Years kicks it all off and it feels like a primal scream of anger at the various injustices Ziggy encounters as the earth careers towards impending doom. It's a bit of a list song that builds beautifully to a crescendo. A definite grower that put me in mind of The Waterboys *This Is The Sea* album. Mike Scott's vocal delivery mimicking Bowie's screeching intensity. Bowie is not a singer in a traditional sense. He's a vocal expressionist that isn't always to my taste but on Five Years he nails it.

Soul Love following Five Years just makes me smile. It's a song you could imagine Lou Rawls or Barry White growling over. It's a groove with Bowie again creating a sound that just about works. On Paul Weller's *On Sunset* he does something similar on the track More. How it fits into a concept like Ziggy Stardust I'm not quite sure. I'm happy for someone to explain. It's a lovely song, a phrase I wasn't expecting to use.

Moonage Daydream is all kinds of mad. It's a heavy metal vibe that instantly put me in mind of The Cult. To my ears Ian Astbury is another devotee to the school of Bowie vocal acrobatics. The bit I love most, though, is the middle eight that reminds me of those hippy lunchtime children's TV programmes from the 70s like *Pipkins*, *Fingermouse* or *Bod*. It shouldn't have any right to be plonked in the middle of a freeform ramble of lyrics and guitar but there it is. Bowie's influence on children's TV is a whole new subject for another day.

Starman then. A massive hit that I'm obviously familiar with. Should Bowie songs ever come up as a question on *Pointless* I suspect Starman would be the worst answer. Everyone knows it. It's great, luscious, melodic and everything you'd expect when Bowie ventures into space. Listening to it as often as I have, though, one thing struck me; Noel Gallagher has lifted the intro and beat for a number of plodding Oasis songs scattering his monodust on it where Bowie sprinkled Stardust. I hope I haven't ruined it for you.

It Ain't Easy is one of those songs that from the first line I visualised another band from the future, 30 years into the future, performing the song. I can see the video, see the performers, the flashing monochrome lighting, crashing through the song in a mix of guitar showmanship and simplistic drumming. Man and woman, husband and wife. You got it yet? Of course you have. It's Jack and Meg, The White Stripes. It's so familiar I even searched the internet to try and find it. I was so close. There's a YouTube clip of Jack doing it live with The Raconteurs. The song is a force of nature. I love it.

Lady Stardust is a return to the theatrical Bowie of previous albums. An androgynous tale performed with a mix of light touch and gusto. The "Alrights" would appear again in *Young Americans* . Continuing the vocal mimicry theme there are moments where it could be Jon Bon Jovi dressed as a cowboy with his six string across his back singing a song from a Western. It's another lovely song. That's it. Lovely.

Star to me is a straight up rock pop tune that I didn't expect to find on an album that's so revered. I'm delighted it's there. I have a real soft spot for mid 70s pop songs and one of the first records I bought as a child was Glass of Champagne by Sailor. The piano from that was clearly lifted directly from Star. It feels like it inspired bands like The Motors, Racey and Jigsaw. If that is the case then it's a Bowie legacy that's right up my street. It's a belter.

Hang On To Yourself takes us back to the rock 'n' roll era and also forward to a pub rock, punk, new wave stomp along. It's Dave Edmunds Queen Of Hearts meets Sham 69. A fantastic song full of spirit and energy but like Star not what I expected to find on *Ziggy Stardust*.

Ziggy Stardust is another stone cold classic. One of those songs that I would have loved to have been around to experience at the time like Hound Dog or Hey Joe. It must have been astonishing to witness in 1972. Where the look and sound meet in perfect harmony. Minds blown, drugs taken, experiences experienced. I suspect Justin Hawkins and The Darkness along with many others found inspiration in such an iconic song musically and in performance. I really have nothing new to add here it's everything popular music should be.

Suffragette City - another familiar song sent me off to actually do some research into the lyrics and meaning. It would appear he's referring to a person rather than a place in an overtly sexual manner. He's on his Suffragette City and she's outta sight, she's alright. Nope, not a clue what he's on about but there are thousands of words out there on the subject. The sound was familiar to me. My older sisters weren't huge Beatles fans but they did own Back In The USSR which is very similar in feel to Suffragette City but I guess if you're going to borrow from someone.

Rock 'n' Roll Suicide closes the album and it takes us back to the beginning with more chest beating cries of anguish over an acoustic arrangement. The overall feeling of the song took me back again to the 2000s and the self-proclaimed indie kings of the time, Razorlight. It's just the kind of thing Johnny Borrell would have thrived on. Standing naked to the waist, in the spotlight, believing he was the second coming. In his dreams. Twat. In Bowie's hands, though, it's a great finish and his "You're not alone" is spine-tingling. That voice of his is a real conundrum.

So, in conclusion, I was expecting a concept album full of great songs that matched Bowie,s latest incarnation. In parts it really is remarkable. In others it's just a decent rock album leaning on some Hendrix guitar dressed up in a fancy image. I was also expecting to hear influences on the early 80s Blitz kids but it appears they just borrowed the clothes. The musical inspiration from *Ziggy Stardust* went from mid 70s pop to 2000s indie, via Brit Pop. I just wish I could have heard it in 1972 the day after he did Starman on *Top Of The Pops*. I expect you really had to be there. If you were, please let me know how it felt. It's an experience I'd like to hear all about. A final thought. It was recorded at almost the same time as *Hunky Dory*. For me they could have made one absolutely phenomenal album from the best of the songs from both albums. Surely Life on Mars at least belongs on *Ziggy Stardust*? Regardless *Ziggy* joins *Hunky Dory* on a list of albums I'll return to.

Comments from The Afterword

Hugh Janus says

21/03/2021 at 13:25

Good old Bowie. You can rely on him to divide opinions and that's exactly how he would have wanted it. I'd have left off Soul Love for a start, mainly because it doesn't quite seem to fit in. I felt the same about It Ain't Easy. Best track – Moonage Daydream, almost for the line, "I'm an alligator" alone. I really don't get Ronson though; his solo on the live video while Bowie goes off to change clothes, sounds like somebody who has never played a guitar before in their life, has been invited up onto the stage to make as much noise as possible. Surely he must have deliberately de-tuned his guitar to achieve the gonzo effect, which sounds like a woman whining on and on in a broad Stamfordonian accent.

I think Hunky Dory is at least its equal and insome respects has dated rather better. To make it near-perfect I'd have left off Fill Your Heart and substituted either the beautiful Letter To Hermione, or ideally, if sufficient room, the remarkable Cygnet Committe off the Space Oddity album. It's interesting to hear Dave Amitri's take on it though, through ears uninfluenced by the context of its time.

deramdaze says

21/03/2021 at 11:27

Starman is on TOTP before the album, EVERYONE adores it and talks about it the following day, so it obviously gets to no. 1 or is thwarted by Slade or Rod Stewart and has to settle for no. 2... only, no, that didn't happen as it only just scrapes into the Top 10.

I think the vast majority of the memories of the performance are retrospective ones.

Vulpes Vulpes says

21/03/2021 at 11:49

Hang on, I'm just going to spin up the nice CD reissue from a few years back and have a wallow. You've made me want to listen again, Dave. I was 17, doing my A levels, when it came out, and it was, for me and my friends, a really important album. Two or three years later I was still clubbing with a mate who went by the name of 'Ziggy', dressed the role, and had a lightning flash and all the eye makeup. I can't for the life of me remember his real name now, but his devotion was indicative of the impact the record had. Provincial boys out at the weekend trying to pick up girls (or boys) and having a blast – and now we had our own hero to sing along with. Great times.

dai says

21/03/2021 at 13:28

Nice write up. I think one of the greatest albums ever made. Some seem to prefer Aladdin Sane from this period, but to my mind Ziggy is very very close to perfection. Only thing I might change is to put John I'm Only Dancing on it instead of the cover version. Starman could be his greatest song.

Twang says

21/03/2021 at 16:00

I was there, saw the TOTP appearance and immediately bought the single. I didn't have the money for the album but my aunt had it and my mum, during a visit, taped it for me off the record player speaker with a mono cassette player as you did back then. She was visiting with my younger brother who appeared briefly on the tape asking "mum, where's my socks" just as the sax solo starts in Soul Love. For years after when I heard the CD I expected his voice to appear. I loved it and know every note, and went on to love Aladdin Sane too, then suddenly decided he was a bit silly and have only had passing interest since.

For more comments or to join the conversation go to https://theafterword.co.uk/12-bowie-albums-in-12-months-the-rise-and-fall-of-ziggy-stardust-and-the-spiders-from-mars/

Month 4

April 17th

Aladdin Sane

As I reach the fourth month of 12 Bowie albums in 12 months, I find myself at *Aladdin Sane.* Another character change, some very striking iconic make up and another collection of eclectic styles and sounds for a first-time listener to discover. I'll not deny that scanning the track listing and just recognising The Jean Genie I felt my first pang of Bowie fatigue and to be honest the first listen left me a little nonplussed. However, what I have discovered with Bowie is that there is always something in one of these albums. A hook, a sound, a hint of recognition or even an annoyance that gives me the impetus to continue. After a couple more listens I came up with the phrase "It's a bit David Quoie". I'm not sure it's unique but I'm claiming it for the number of three chord boogie tunes that litter the album. Then there's the piano, lots of piano, more on that later. Finally, it's a very, very 70s album. "Of course it is Dave," I hear you cry. In fact it's so specifically 70s that in order to try something different to shake things up a bit I've turned the whole review into a reimagination of an early 70s episode of Top of the Pops, with some artistic licence to keep the pedants pedanting. Please indulge me here as I settle down with my family one Thursday evening in 1973. Mum knitting and dad looking over the top of his paper. Older sisters hoping for a performance from David Essex. Me and my brother hoping that Pan's People don't embarrass us all either with what they're not wearing or their painfully literal interpretation of the songs. The show begins.

DLT is presenting and as is the way of these things the first song is an upbeat foot stomper. **Watch That Man** to me is every inch a Rod Stewart and The Faces tune. A bluesy rock and roll number that is a great start to the show. In my head I can picture Rod and Ron Wood, heads together over a single mike miming the Watch That Man lyric as Rod spins away to muck about at the back of the stage. A strong start. Dad didn't lift his head above the paper but Mum sneaked a cheeky peak at Rod's bum.

Back to DLT now who puts a serious face on and declares "now for something very special..." of course it's **Aladdin Sane** and I nearly went with Steely Dan for this, there's little hints towards it being a Dan tune. On reflection though you can't have a Bowie album reimagined without having one Bowie performance. So here we are. This is such a Bowie song and in my imaginary *Top Of The Pops* this would be the performance of the night. Confusing my dad and sending him to the kitchen for a cup of tea. My sisters giggling at the bulges in the skin tight trousers and me and my brother not quite understanding what was going on but knowing we'd be talking about it in the playground tomorrow. It's a brilliant song. The play on the phrase "a lad insane", so creative, inventive, druggy and dreamy. Right up my alley. Yet in the spirit of honesty it's slightly ruined for me by Mike Garson's freeform jazz piano that sounds like a set of off-key church bells. I think I'd prefer a radio edit but that's my problem. I realise it is hugely important to Bowie heads so I won't mention Les Dawson here as that would be disrespectful. This is the David Bowie I was hoping to find. It's rarer though than the fandom would have me believe.

It's all too much for DLT as he mock fans his hirsute face while the kids jockey for position. His enthusiasm wanes as he realises its *Top Of The Pops* stalwarts Mud next. Again. Doing **Drive In Saturday.** Dressed in their teddy boy gear they phone in a performance of the fourth single from their album knowing no one except my dad is listening and cursing the producers for putting them on after Bowie. Yet as we know this is a Bowie song in reality and we're all wondering what it's doing here and how you go from Aladdin Sane to this half-arsed ode to 50s life.

DLT is clearly back on his game as he readies himself for his next link. Introducing **Panic In Detroit** by informing us that Deep Purple can't be in the studio tonight but Pan's People are here. Their performance consists of walking then running around a cardboard city, wearing very little and panicking, looking shocked with hands waving above their heads. You get the picture. Dad's put his paper down and mum's angry clicking nearly drowns out the TV. I love the song actually. Raucous, with a driving beat and a great vocal. A heavy metal tune with a splash of Bowie drama. Superb.

At this point in 1973 DLT would have uttered "Phwoar" and mopped his brow or something equally inappropriate and gone on to announce **Cracked Actor** which for my imaginary *Top Of The Pops* is performed by T Rex. It doesn't stretch the imagination too far as it's a meat and two veg glam rock anthem. Bolan or Bowie, it passes us all by. Dad's snoring now and a fight has broken out between me and my brother over the last orange Matchmaker.

DLT is now standing alone as the mood in the studio drops. "And now time for something a little bit different. From the new Andrew Lloyd Webber musical *Time* it's **Time** performed by David Essex." My sisters move to the edge of the sofa, mum puts her knitting down "he's got lovely eyes" and me, my brother and my dad start talking football. At least that's my take on perhaps the most theatrical of all the Bowie songs I've heard so far. It's a straight up musical theatre tune, from the delivery to the almost spoken part, the musicality. Like something from *Evita* or *Chess*. Did he write a musical? Maybe he should have, it's clear the will for dramatic musical theatre was there but does it belong here?

Next up, crashing into the charts is that other bunch of fake teddy boys straight from the fancy dress cupboard with **The Prettiest Star**. It's Showaddywaddy. Doowopping, finger clicking and synchronised stepping along to a slowed down rock 'n' roll rhythm from times past. My sisters are planning to recreate the moves with their mates in the playground tomorrow. Dad becomes animated and joins in the finger clicking. "Aha, a proper tune," he announces. Back in the real world, how this song aligns itself with the image Bowie was projecting at the time is beyond me. I'm clearly missing something here.

DLT back announces it as a "future number one" and introduces **Let's Spend The Night Together** informing us it's a cover of The Rolling Stones classic (thank god he's here). Who have I selected in my imaginary Thursday night pop fest for this? Of course it's Status Quo. Legs apart, head to foot in denim, nodding along to an all too familiar song with absolutely nothing added. It's great fun. We get up and head bang along. It annoys mum and dad but this from the great innovator? Baffling again.

Coming towards the end of the show now and DLT announces a new number one. **The Jean Genie** by Sweet. Now this is the most obvious of my imaginary musings. The song is so similar to Blockbuster that we must assume one copied the other but apparently not. Both recorded on the same label, at approximately the same time, using the same riff and from what

I can discover it was pure coincidence missed by the A & R man. Ironically Blockbuster got to number one and The Jean Genie didn't. The Jean Genie remains one of Bowie's most commercial tunes and one I really like. It's everything a glam rock song should be. Driving, rocking, over the top and best played loud. This is Bowie to me. Me and my brother want to buy it from Woolies at the weekend.

Back in the day *Top Of The Pops* would play out with a song over the credits. This week it's **Lady Grinning Soul** which DLT informs us is from the latest Bond film. I'm stretching my time lines here at making it Shirley Bassey because it deserves a proper singer. Bowie does a great job of it and it's easily my favourite song on the album. It's a beautiful, swoon of a song. Delicious and light with a hint of drama. A lovely, lovely end.

So, what does my lighthearted bit of nonsense mean? It means *Aladdin Sane* is an album of incredible highs and some inexplicable song choices. Bowie was a master at dressing up something familiar in some fancy clothes and make up and selling it as the future. The bands I referenced all had great commercial success yet were hardly at the cutting edge of popular music. There's a pattern forming for me; when he's great he's everything I expected and more but to justify his exalted place in the history of popular music are there just far too many "shrug" songs you can just take or leave? The four albums I've covered so far were released in a two-year period, April '71 to April '73. Did that effect the quality control? I maintain he could have made two mind blowing albums in the same period but Bowie heads will tell me he made four and not to be such a dick. Aladdin Sane is an enjoyable listen but overall the Bowie legend remains an unsolved mystery to me.

Comments From The Afterword

Black Celebration says

17/04/2021 at 19:51

Wonderfully funny review – Panic in Detroit as interpreted by Pans People is right on the money. I thought it was beyond doubt that the JG riff had been nicked for Blockbuster.I did read that there was a confrontation between Bowie and Sweet's producer when they had a chance meeting. The story goes that Bowie approaches him, is stony-faced, uses the C-word and then breaks into a big smile and offers warm congratulations for their number one.

Black Type says

17/04/2021 at 21:17

The riff for both songs was ripped off from The Yardbirds' I'm A Man which was ripped off from Bo Diddley's, which was adapted from Muddy Waters', etc etc. They were created at roughly the same time on different sides of the Atlantic. Just serendipity.

NigelT says

17/04/2021 at 20:14

I think you're pretty much on the money. I've had it since the 70's and it's intriguing that a new listenr over 40 years later should come to the same conclusion – I have always thought it sounded a bit thrown together and rushed. The cover art is superb though, isn't it?

nickduvet says

17/04/2021 at 22:47

Great review Dave, the best so far. You've pretty much nailed it, but while your description of Drive-in Saturday as a "half arsed ode to 50's life" had me spluttering into my coffee, you've missed the mark on that one. It was the 60s (Jagger, Twig the wonder kid, etc). One of his best songs too

MC Escher says

18/04/2021 at 07:15

The review is wonderful conceit and the choice of acts you have covering the songs is inspired . Kudos for the LGS Bond theme idea too, I've always thought exactly the same. Give the title track some more time though: that piano solo is possibly the greatest in pop music.

Arthur Cowslip says

19/04/2021 at 06:10

I think you are a little bit harsh on this album. When I was discovering Bowie in the early 90s, I liked aladdin more than ziggy. I think it sounds meatier and much more assured in its sense of experimentation and playfulness than his earlier albums. He sounds like the proper space commander he was born to be, and not merely a rock singer/songwriter any more.

fitterstoke says

19/04/2021 at 08:22

I agree…the singles are great, the piano tracks are really superb, Ronno and Mike Garson are on fire, each in their own way…and Bowie is imperious.

My views expressed in Dave's review threads to date make me sound like a contrarian, just going against the received wisdom (MWSTW and Aladdin Sane seriously under-rated; Hunky Dory and Ziggy slightly over-rated) – I guess it depends where your head is when you first hear these LPs…

Diddley Farquar says

20/04/2021 at 11:31

I listened to the album this morning. I like it better than Ziggy because it's more loose, there's room for a bit more improvisation, like on the title track. The tracks I find less interesting are those most like the album before. It's also all so rock 'n' roll really, as was glam rock and much other music of that era, often quite retro. I don't think I like Mick Ronson's guitar sound at times. It's got a bit of the ugly glam rock sound, occasionally evoking the glitter band for instance, or Sweet, elsewhere, like on Prettiest Star, it is almost unpleasantly sharp, piercing. I am more of a post-Ronson Bowie admirer really, 76-80. But the best of this album is really fantastic, Aladdin Sane,

Drive In Saturday, Let's Spend The Night Together. Time is more of the theatrical, could have been in a rock musical like Rocky Horror, type of thing. Good tune though, in parts.

For more comments and to join the conversation go to https://theafterword.co.uk/12-bowie-albums-in-12-months-aladdin-sane/

Month 5

May 17th

Pinups

Month five of 12 Bowie albums in 12 months brings me to *Pinups* Another striking piece of cover art featuring Bowie and Twiggy looking like a couple of mime artists fresh from Covent Garden, their faces frozen in a mixture of melancholy and terror. It puts me in mind of an old Word Blog collection of photos depicting "Pop Stars Breaking Wind". Twiggy is clearly the guilty guffer here and Bowie the horrified guffee. Anyway, enough of that, on to the album.

A collection of covers from various bands from the 60s and 70s. I knew of some of the originals, others were completely new to me. When writing the other pieces in this project, I've been able to rely heavily on influence and connections I've heard through Bowie's music whether it was Bowie being the influencer or being influenced, guffer or guffee as it were. This collection of songs makes that really tough because they are all covers and for the first time all pretty much of the same style. The overriding feeling I got on the first few listens was that the style here was "Pub Rock". Three years before the "Pub Rock" scene really took off, Bowie had decided to leave his characters behind causing some consternation among his "Spiders From Mars" band mates and under record company pressure for an album, chose twelve songs to record over two months. I love this snippet from the album booklet that I found while doing some reading on the album.

"These songs are among my favourites from the '64-67' period of London. Most of the groups were playing the Ricky-Tick (was it a ‘y’ or an ‘i’?) scene club circuit (Marquee, eel pie island la la). Some are still with us. Pretty Things, Them, Yardbirds, Syd’s Pink Floyd, Mojos, Who, Easybeats, Merseys, The Kinks. Love on ya!”

Had Bowie invented “Pub Rock” or was he following a trend set back in the 60s with bands just trying to catch a break? Had he tapped in to a scene? Was it just a lazy throw away filler? Was it actually a catharsis, a break from the old showie Bowie hiding behind a fancy image? Maybe I’ll find out when I move on to *Diamond Dogs*. He was top of his commercial game at the time with *Pinups* becoming his sixth album in the charts. Whatever it was it feels very different to what I’ve covered so far. In fact, it has a feel of a live album and may well have been better for it. So I’m going to ask you to imagine a seedy, smoky, sticky carpet of indeterminate colour pub with a small stage in Camden or Hammersmith or some such in 1973. A clientele dressed like extras from *The Sweeney* on a Friday night looking for some action and some live music and stumbling across this band with the slightly odd front man. “Is that a fella?” Coming on to the stage and about to rip through one of the best nights out you’ve never had.

Rosalyn is a fantastic opener. Pure rock ‘n’ roll catching the crowd’s attention and convincing them that this lot can do it and they’ll be able to leave the pub in one piece. Even the weirdo. A few more pints of light and bitter to be downed as the crowd moved towards the stage to catch some more and then.

They go straight into **Here Comes The Night.** Bowie nearly loses his crowd with the caterwauling wooahs at the start. Nervous looks among the band as the heavies at the front stop nodding along and stare with a “What the fuck?” look in their eyes but the band turns things around, especially the sax man and they're off again with another meat and two veg standard that veers off the path but keeps the punters happy. Two songs in and they've earned some credit in the bank.

I Wish You Would, with its heavy metal riffs and Bowie's vocal really working takes things off to another level and a couple of fights break out as beer gets spilled and the nodding turns to more aggressive movements. You could never call it dancing. I really love this and want to be in that pub right now with an Embassy Number 1 on the go and a pint of Watneys looking like Jack Regan on a night off.

See Emily Play becomes a bit of a jazz/prog freak out but they need to get back to the bar and it passes pretty much unnoticed thanks to some inspired drumming. They kept all the songs around three minutes, going for over four here could have caused a riot, but a barrel needed changing and they've got away with it.

Everything's Alright gets the place jumping again another heavy metal ripsnorter that builds and builds to, bizarrely, a Beatlesque "wooooo" at the end.

I Can't Explain is a familiar tune over and done in just over two minutes which seems a bit pointless but the crowd are into it now and he can't possibly lose them. Can he?

They storm through **Friday On My Mind**.

There's one for the ladies with **Sorrow**. All the lads go for a slash trying to maintain their "laddish" thoughts while actually wondering if they fancy the singer. This just makes them angrier and drink and smoke more, god help their girlfriends tonight.

They return to the brilliant **Don't Bring Me Down** that almost brings the house down. Classic pub rock that ticks every single box.

The lads are fired up now, what's next, these lads can really play. What a night. "COME ON!!!" And then it happens, Bowie does what Bowie does with **Shapes Of Things**. He goes full-on musical theatre and a riot breaks out. Tables smashed, glasses thrown and bottles broken. Police are called and it's like the wild west as the band play on. The landlord calls over "Play something normal for fucks sake, what is this shit!!". Bowie plays on to the last note, he's changing for no one.

Then finishes the set with a storming **Anyway, Anyhow, Anywhere** and brings the crowd back to earth with **Where Have all The Good Times Gone?**. Last orders called and everyone goes home happy. What a night, they'll be back next week.

It's a brilliant album for me bringing to mind Dr Feelgood, Kilburn and the High Roads, The Blockheads, The Motors and even The Jam on The Who covers. Did Deep Purple ever play a pub? If they did, that's in there too. I'm too young to really remember Pub Rock in its pomp but my older sister's first husband, Colin, was a drummer in a band, more wedding than pub but he dressed like he meant it. Sort of 70s snooker meets Sweeney with a serious moustache under a mop of dark hair. Colin was a huge fan of Cozy Powell but my memories of him rehearsing are very much 1-2-3-4, tshhh....

My one real experience of pub rock was Rick Astley (yes I'm going there, stay with me) and his band The Luddites at The Grey Horse in Kingston in 2011. He played drums and hammered his way through a set of rock covers from Neil Young to Kings of Leon. It was brilliant. You could sense it was blowing the cobwebs off those early songs, more catharsis. Playing to 100 people in a dingy pub before reinventing himself and moving on to become the king of Magic FM. So I'm left wondering if *Pinups* was a pivotal moment in Bowie's career. I'll find out next month. *Pinups* is great, maybe only let down by the lack of power in Bowie's vocal but he gets away with it and his insistence at overplaying it even in a 3-minute romp. Whisper it quietly but I think it's my favourite, most complete Bowie album so far.

Comments From The Afterword

Rigid Digit says

17/05/2021 at 19:29

Not just me the who thinks of this album as a bunch of Pub Rock covers. I suggested this once to a couple of Bowie worshipping friends. "Don't be a silly-billy" was their printable response

Lodestone of Wrongness says

17/05/2021 at 20:17

I bought it at the time when I couldn't buy many records due to an almost total lack of money. Consequently I spent many a month forcing myself to like it when I should have been saying "This album is a bunch of Pub Rock covers". Eventually I gave it to Alison as a birthday present. She too was not impressed.

Colin H says

17/05/2021 at 22:21

I hadn't thought of a pub rock comparison before, but you might have something. It's the only Dave album I like. Haven't heard it in years, though – but I still 'hear' it in my mind. Must listen to it properly tomorrow.

Jackthebiscuit says

18/05/2021 at 08:52

FWIIW, I thought/think Pin ups was/is a terrific album & I don't think there is a duff song or note on it.

I still listen to & enjoy it to this day.

Brilliant record.

Tiggerlion says

18/05/2021 at 09:36

I agree.

I've come to realise it's an album that bends time. In 1973 it was looking back, affectionately, to the mid-sixties. The mid-sixties seemed further away then than eighties do now. I once put together a playlist of the originals (or, at least the covers being covered). They all have that characteristic feel of the sixties, whereas Pinups sounds as if it comes from the future, performed by a band that really did come from Mars.

Mick Ronson's fuzzy guitar growls like a muzzled Rottweiler, retooled by a machine. Bowie plays a lot of saxophone throughout, something I can't recall hearing him doing before or since. He is surprisingly accomplished. Credit to Ken Fordham, too. The saxophone is traditionally associated with fifties rock and roll, yet here, it is another exotic, alien ingredient from a different space and time.

It doesn't matter that it is a covers album as most listeners hadn't heard the previous versions anyway. That was certainly true of the teenage me. There is such a genuine love of the songs. The enthusiasm is infectious, giving the whole album a buzz of energy, so much so that one song crashes into another unable to wait its turn.

I'm convinced that Pinups is Bowie's most extraordinary vocal performance, too. He squeals, he yelps, he snarls, he croons. He's having fun and he's fantastic. Yes. There are times when he takes the piss with his vocal (Here Comes The Night's caterwauling, Friday On My Mind's vowel mangling). He's also focussed and intense (I Wish You Would, Everything's Alright, Don't Bring Me Down), wildly experimental (See Emily Play's Bewley Brother's goblins, Shape Of Thing's phasing) and gentle and romantic (Sorrow and Where Have All The Good Times Gone). Take I Can't Explain, for example. Slowed down, stripped of The Who's confused lust and driven by a wheezing sax, it is a touching performance, a croon. The sighing backing vocals, slight echo on the drum kit and presence of a tambourine nod to Spector's wall of sound. It's beautiful.

Add to that, Aynsley Dunbar's tidy drumming, Trevor Bolder's boisterous bass (nicely 'up' in the 2015 mix), Mike Garson's keyboard flourishes and judicious, elegant strings, you have, as you say, Jack, a brilliant album, as you say, Jack, a brilliant album.

dai says

18/05/2021 at 12:01

Nah, horrible arrangements and in pretty much all cases the originals are superior. Completely disposable. I like some of his many covers though on other albums.

For me it's a 2/5 album, come on David you can do better than this!

Timbar says

18/05/2021 at 17:31

I'm really enjoying these reviews. It's giving a fresh perspective on albums I've known for decades – It's also had me looking through some old Bowie biographies to get some more factual details.

Pin Ups was Mick Ronson's favourite Bowie album that he worked on "That album was great to do, because the songs were our favourites when we were teenagers" while Mike Garson had never heard the originals "To me it was just another record to play on that I could contribute my style to"

For Trevor Bolder it was not such fun. He was only invited to play after Jack Bruce had turned the gig down & was warned by Ronson to "keep my mouth shut or I wouldn't be working, because David would get rid of me as well" (Woody Woodmansey was fired on the day of his wedding, which Bolder described as "complete spite")

They chose 12 songs & went into the studio (Chateau d'Herouville) with just the chords & glammed them up. Sorrow is the only one with a big Ronson string arrangement, which were also recorded in Paris.

Island Records were not too pleased with Bowie copying Bryan Ferry's idea for a covers album (These Foolish Things was recorded in June) & some suggest that they were going to sue – They can't have been too happy that there were photos of a sharp suited Mr Bowie holding a sax like Andy Mackay, nor that some of Sorrow's vocal mannerisms were reminiscent of the Roxy Music front man.

Delving further into the biogs does give some more prosaic reasons for Pin Ups. After 2 years of non stop performing & promotion, Bowie was burnt out & an album of covers saved him having to write anything. It also was an opportunity for Mainman to buy back his publishing (He's retired from performing & is now recording covers – the well is dry)

Pin Ups is very much a stop gap, the last of the glam albums, but also the sound of Bowie, Ronson & co having fun.

For more comments and to join the conversation go to https://theafterword.co.uk/12-bowie-albums-in-12-months-pin-ups/

Month 6

June 18th

Diamond Dogs

And in the death
As the last few corpses lay rotting on the slimy
Thoroughfare
The shutters lifted in inches in Temperance Building
High on Poacher's Hill
And red, mutant eyes gaze down on Hunger City
No more big wheels

Fleas the size of rats sucked on rats the size of cats
And ten thousand peoploids split into small tribes
Coverting the highest of the sterile skyscrapers
Like packs of dogs assaulting the glass fronts of Love-Me Avenue
Ripping and rewrapping mink and shiny silver fox, now
legwarmers
Family badge of sapphire and cracked emerald
Any day now
The Year of the Diamond Dogs

This ain't Rock'n'Roll
This is Genocide

And so it begins with **Future Legend**. My ears prick, my pulse quickens, here we go. This is the time where Bowie becomes more than fancy clothes, cover versions and rehashed rock 'n' roll. The crazy motherfucker is going to take me on a wild ride here. Hang on to your hat Dave.

Except, the next song **Diamond Dogs** is just another Rolling Stones sound alike. I didn't imagine when watching Bowie and

Jagger "Dancin' In The Street" in 1985 that 26 years later I'd be writing how Bowie had nicked Jagger's act in 1974. I know Bowie heads will tut and explain how I don't understand but how do you go from that edgy narration of an apocalyptic vision of a dystopian future inhabited by "peopleoids" to that and not think "I really should be doing better than this". Because he does do far better than that later on in the album, much better. Maybe it's just that the track ordering in *Diamond Dogs* is clearly just wrong. More on that in my final summary.

The song **Diamond Dogs** is OK, a decent Rolling Stones tune with some freaky lyrics continuing the theme but this is David Bowie in 1974 and from what I've read and what people have told me I expect so much more.

Anyway, on to **Sweet Thing** which is a lovely song, sung beautifully, and with its reprise following the slightly heavier **Candidate** it's what this album should be about. It's theatrical in that now familiar Bowie way. Hardly surprising as I've read that it was one of the songs he'd had in mind for his musical based on Orwell's 1984 for which he was denied permission by Orwell's wife. More on that later, bloody stupid running order.

Rebel Rebel next. While being familiar to me again just sounds like The Rolling Stones. Maybe there's an intentional link I'm not aware of but Bowie the plagiarist was not what I was expecting. So frustrating, I want to be thrilled by Bowie. I want to feel what others feel yet 6 albums in it still all feels a bit of a rock 'n' roll swindle.

However, I've committed to this and if I've learned anything with these albums it's that every time I feel I'm running out of steam, Bowie finds something to pique my interest and **Rock 'n' Roll With Me** does just that. It's a song with just about every

MOR trick in the book thrown in, from Manilow to Bon Jovi it should be the song the radio, hit loving Bowie fans adore but you just don't hear it in the mainstream. Yet it is possibly the most mainstream Bowie song I think I've heard. It's as far from the apocalypse as an episode of Mr Tumble but I actually like it. I can imagine a sea of big haired mid 80s kids waving their lighters in the air as Jon Bon Jovi and Richie Sambora close out a show at some enormodome with it. How it fits here? I don't know. Anyone?

Oh right, now we're back to the apocalypse with **We Are The Dead;** a funeral march that goes nowhere but at least fits the theme, if indeed there is a theme as it's so all over the place. Nothing more really to add to this song, it's just there, doing its thing.

Now what happens next was a complete surprise to me, from nowhere on the back of some hair rock and a dirge we get the next two songs from his 1984 trilogy. They are absolutely brilliant. THIS is what I was expecting. From the little I've read Bowie was seriously upset at not being given permission to write his 1984 musical. Let me tell you, so am I because if this was the standard it may well have ended up being his finest piece of work. It's really clear that he was desperate to write a stage musical; he's a performer first and foremost, creating images and characters and themes but never really following it through. The song **1984** has possibly become my favourite. It fits my pop sensibilities like a glove, sounding like Papa Was A Rolling Stone and Theme From 'Shaft' for the theatre sung by Ian McNabb doing Love Is A Wonderful Colour. Imagine an album or a show full of this stuff. It goes straight into **Big Brother** which kicks of like a Tubeway Army song that Gary Numan would have died for. It grows and grows into everything you'd want from a Bowie song with hooks and a Sgt Pepperesque mid section with brass before breaking into a spine-tingling vocal I didn't know Bowie was capable of. The two songs are an absolute triumph.

The album ends with **Chant of the Ever Circling Skeletal Family**. Nope, me neither. It's a bit of a nothing ending but the fact it ends like the start of The Jam's Trans Global Express is a twist that works for me.

So where does that leave me and my relationship with Bowie? Confused, frustrated and a little disappointed. He touches such great heights here, up there with Starman and Life on Mars, but somehow he's yet to create the perfect album for me. I am starting to wonder if the real Bowie heads just sort of ignore the meat and two veg elements to focus on the intricate delicacies that are there if you look for them. The radio listening Bowie lovers are clearly content with the hits. I've listened to this on Spotify. Staggeringly Rebel Rebel has 220 million listens while the majestic 1984 and Big Brother have 5 million between them. That's quite a disparity. Those two songs are clearly, obviously, absolutely more worthy of reaching more ears than Rebel Rebel. This from a man who found worth in the Thomspon Twins by the way so maybe it's me. Either way if this album had got the two Stones tracks out of the way early, opening with Rebel Rebel, then the MOR Rock 'n'Roll With Me and ended on the apocalyptic stuff from Future Legends, through We Are The Dead, Sweet Thing then the 1984 stuff I think it would have made for a far more coherent and listenable experience.

So can I after 6 albums offer a couple of thoughts? Firstly, if Bowie had focussed solely on his space obsession, his need to make musical theatre and his love of rock 'n' roll and released three albums over the same period concentrating on those elements, could he have achieved even greater acclaim? I'm really desperately sorry that 1984 the musical wasn't completed. I think a space song album would have been just out of this world (sorry) and a straight up rock 'n' roll album could have been a right laugh. A *Pinups* of Bowie songs perhaps.

Secondly was Bowie acutely aware of this and so wrapped each release up in mystery, make up, fancy clothes and a story to throw us off the scent? I found this quote from him on *Diamond Dogs*:

"I was looking to create a profligate world that could have been inhabited by characters from Kurt Weill or John Rechy – that sort of atmosphere. A bridge between Enid Blyton's Beckenham and The Velvet Underground's New York. Without Noddy, though."

Was he really serious, was he playing up to the arty types and the hipsters while laughing at us and himself? Ultimately, what I think matters not a jot and anyway it's just music. I am truly desperate to love Bowie and parts of this album make that happen but then others leave me searching for the skip button.

Comments From The Afterword

Junior Wells says

18/06/2021 at 12:56

Another good un Dave. Possibly my favourite along with a few you are yet to review. Do Bowieites ignore his meat and 2 veg songs? No. The other option is we like them. Dissing DD and RR as just Rolling Stones soundalikes could just as easily been described as songs the Stones would love to have written.

Tiggerlion says

18/06/2021 at 15:46

There are very strong rumours Jagger and Bowie had a sexual relationship. They were inseparable for months. Angie (does the name ring any bells) once found them asleep together, naked. There are plenty of Stones references on Aladdin Sane, including a cover version. Bowie saw Jagger as the ultimate Rock star, probably more so than Iggy because Jagger was fantastically successful. They fell out over Guy Peelleart. Jagger had his work on his walls as he was thinking of using him for the cover of It's Only Rock & Roll. Bowie immediately phoned him up and Diamond Dogs beat the Stones to it.

Rebel Rebel is deliberately Stones like. The riff actually out-does anything the Stones could come up with at the time. Bowie wanted to prove to the Rock fans than he wasn't just fey. He wanted to rock harder than The Sweet or Slade in a song he saw as his 'farewell' (two fingered?) to Glam. Of course, he couldn't help himself and wrote the lyric with the gender bending right in your face. It's a magnificent fist-pumping record. A great single.

Keith was unimpressed. Bowie had joined in handclaps for a Stones recording session at Jagger's invitation. Keith took great pleasure in removing every single one the following day.

Another thought-provoking review, Dave. Thumbs up!

Timbar says

18/06/2021 at 16:24

It was during that time, when Bowie & Jagger were hanging out, that they went to Ronnie Wood's one night & recorded the rough of It's only Rock n Roll

"Help me with this one. I've got this chorus & these verses" said Jagger.

Bowie + Wood provided the backing vocals, along with Willie Weeks on bass & Kenney Jones on drums.

Keith said they tried recutting it, "but in the end we said keep the original, and we'll overdub, because it's got the feel."

I don't know if this was before or after Bowie wrote/recorded the song Diamond Dogs, but he did quote "it's only rock n roll" when singing it live.

Dave Amitri (aka Dave Ross) says

19/06/2021 at 10:40

Thanks @tiggerlion and @timbar these moments when my ill informed guesswork is somehow half way accurate (the same Elton piano thing still blows my mind) is the closest I ever get to feeling smug.

Didn't think for a second that Bowie and Jagger could have been an item, mind blown again.

Diddley Farquar says

19/06/2021 at 10:54

What impresses me is that Bowie managed to fire off at least one all-time great, classic single on every album since probably Hunky Dory, all the way up to and including Let's Dance. Non-single album tracks can be variable but the singles, wow.

Gary says

19/06/2021 at 18:00

I am totes agree. And post Let's Dance I'd add Absolute Beginners and Where Are We Now to the wowers.

But the thing about Bowie is, more than any other pop star - more than any other artist in fact- I'm glad I got to share the planet with him. Quite simply, he made the seventies and eighties so much more colourful. Growing up not knowing where he was going to go next and being delighted most times, not just with some of the music and, obviously, with his changing image but also with the ripples he created throughout popular culture and elsewhere.

For more comments and to join the conversation go to https://theafterword.co.uk/12-bowie-albums-in-12-months-diamond-dogs/

Month 7

July 24th

Young Americans

I've been looking forward to this album since I started this project back in January. I've often heard how it was Billy Mackenzie's favourite Bowie album so I thought this would be full of nods to the weird and wonderful world of The Associates. I asked on "The Affectionate Bunch" The Associates Facebook fan page for opinions and hoped that Alan Rankine may share a story or two. In the end an old friend of Billy's answered.

"I don't know if it was a favourite but I know he took my newly bought Young Americans in King Buyers in Dundee and traded me 2 Sensational Alex Harvey Band LP's"

Which proves something I suppose. Nothing from Alan unfortunately. I tried really hard to find something that linked the album to Billy or The Associates. Maybe one song I'll cover later hinted at some vocal stylisation I recognised but not much more. What I did hear was a sax heavy, smooth, jazzy album that brought to mind artists from the early/mid-eighties being so heavily reliant on female backing singers and a saxophonist. On to the album.

Young Ameicans, the song, is ubiquitous for anyone of a certain age. The "alright's" instantly recognisable even to the most civilian Magic FM listener out there. It's a tremendous song and instantly Bowie but I would suggest a complete departure from what had come before. Poppier, jazzier, instantly radio-friendly yet only number 18 in the UK charts in 1975 when released as a single. The bleak lyrics hidden behind the song's uptempo rhythms and soulful sounds. I can imagine a whole raft of young aspiring pop stars hearing this and thinking "THAT'S the music I want to make. I was thinking maybe Hall and Oates until I checked and realised they were making music in 1975 but still there are some similarities and their peak came a few years later. Boy George would have been 14 when released and you can see how this song would have inspired him. The first five seconds of the intro and I start singing the opening to If You Let Me Stay by Terence Trent D'Arby. That, I think, sets this whole review up as different to the previous ones. There are lots of little hints to what a whole generation of 80s artists heard and carried with them.

The first few bars of **Win** into the backing vocals and Bowie's breathy delivery take me right to 1986 and The Blow Monkey's debut album Animal Magic and particularly Aeroplane City Lovesong. To be honest I could have picked almost any song from the album to register the influence on Dr Robert. Although Win isn't as sax heavy as some of the others the overall feel of the song is just the floaty gorgeousness that The Blow Monkeys excel at. I messaged Dr Robert through Twitter asking if it was fair to say he was influenced by *Young Americans* and he answered "I think it influenced everyone of my generation". Which while not going into any great detail confirms the obvious to anyone who listened to the album and turned on a radio in 1986. It's a beautiful song, pitched just right. Bowies vocal seems less strained than previously and is well suited to the smoother feel. Lovely.

Fascination takes me back to *Starsky and Hutch* and those opening credits but also for some reason that I can't fully explain to 80s Scotland and Orange Juice. There's some Edwyn

Collins styling in Bowie's vocal and the funk guitar and drumming a reminder of What Presence perhaps? It's a slice of funk and soul that may even have got Niles Rodgers thinking. I haven't checked the dates on that one. Listening while the weather has been so hot it just felt right for sweaty, muggy nights, probably more New York than Glasgow but such is the familiarity that I can't quite pin down - it could be anywhere.

Right Is my favourite song on the album. It could have come directly from Paul Weller's *On Sunset* but equally if you use your imagination it's a great lost Style Council song. I can see Weller with a sweater hung casually over his shoulders, while Steve White does his thing with the beat and Weller plays his funk guitar but what seals the Style Council vibe is the DC Lee backing vocals. Remarkable. It's the most obvious "influence" I found on the album. It's a lazy, jazzy, funky thing that if just put on Our Favourite Shop wouldn't need one note changed.

Somebody Up There Likes Me starts with a Gerry Rafferty or Hazel O'Connor sax solo but doesn't really go anywhere after that. Maybe I'm missing something but it doesn't quite work for me.

Across The Universe is where I can perhaps hear some Billy Mackenzie styling in the vocals but in reality I'm not sure where this song is going with it's Hey Jude like repetition. It's a bit of a return to old Bowie.

Can You Hear Me? is back to the blue-eyed soul Bowie which is where he's at his best here. Soft vocals, strings and those delicious backing vocals again. There's something of Colin Vearncombe in the vocal and is another straight out of the "Making a Record in 1986" handbook. It's not a criticism, it's a beautiful song.

Young Americans finishes on **Fame** another of those songs everyone knows. Much like Right being a lost Style Council song, Fame could have come straight off an album by The Kane Gang - just to keep the 80s analogies coming. The slightly staccato feel punctuated by bursts of lyric and little funk segments. I suspect it's a song Grace Jones was familiar with too as it contains elements from Pull Up To The Bumper. A decent ending.

Whether it's me, whether I was expecting too much, whether it really is Bowie fatigue but I feel this review is a bit flat. I've commented how the previous Bowie albums I've reviewed were all crazy mixes of styles which gave me lots to get my teeth into. Maybe Young Americans being a definite style throughout didn't give me anything to rail against or find my own inspiration for. It's a nice album that while I can hear all these sounds that I recognise from some of my absolute favourite artists, to be honest I wouldn't listen to again before any of them. I know this came first and it's clearly a hugely important album that inspired, as Dr Robert said, a whole generation, but I think those that came next did it better overall. I guess being the first doesn't always mean it's the best.

I was looking finally for the album that inspired the heady crazy days of The Blitz, electronic music and all those creative early 80s bands and ultimately found a jazzy, funky smooth slice of blue-eyed soul. I think maybe it's me and maybe I'll stop here as, like this review, I feel quite flat without much enthusiasm for what comes next. Some artists aren't for everyone and trying to find what some of my heroes found has left me frustrated and a little disappointed.

Comments From The Afterword

Nick L says

24/07/2021 at 12:13

As ever, great write up Dave. Personally I always thought it was an OK album spoilt by the inclusion of Across The Universe but I'm sure others will disagree. You can definitely here the influence in a lot of 80's faux soul stuff though, good and bad. I completely agree with your point about not listening to it again over your favourite artists who took influence from it though.

metal mickey says

24/07/2021 at 14:23

Another nice review, thanks Dave, I'm really enjoying your project.

I think it's worth reminding ourselves just how prolific Bowie was back then – YA followed less than 10 months after Diamond Dogs, and the whole thing was basically written & recorded whilst on the road in the US touring the latter album, as DB became enamoured of the new disco & soul sounds he was hearing on American radio... in fact the 2nd leg of the tour was completely re-worked to incorporate these new songs. These albums aren't meant to be magnum opuses carved into stone, they're quick despatches from the DB frontline, as if to say "This is what I'm into at the moment, pop back in 10 months and I'll let you know what's next..."

… and as Black Type alludes to above, Station To Station, the next, er, stop on your Bowie journey might just make you really see what all the DB fuss is about…

Rigid Digit says

24/07/2021 at 16:52

Young Americans is probably my least favourite DB album. It just doesn't "click" with me.

If Diamond Dogs was an attempt (and a successful one) to put Ziggy behind him and establish himself as an artist, then Young Americans was proving to himself that if he put the work in, he could succeed at whatever form took his fancy at the time.

You mention "Bowie Fatigue" – I think that's what Dave was suffering from on this one (this is the point where he survived on orange juice and cocaine isn't it?).

Young Americans presented his current enthusiasm, and once that was out of his system I think he then produced his best 4 albums...

Timbar says

24/07/2021 at 19:23

I've always been a bit underwhelmed by Young Americans. Apart from the two singles that book end the album, the other tracks have never really "stuck" – a strange "dry" production, and an over prominent sax throughout.

David Sanborn said "The way he presented it to me at the outset of the sessions was, 'There's not going to be any lead guitar on this record. There's going to be rhythm guitar and bass and drums and piano. You're going to be the lead guitar.' I didn't really know how that was going to work, but I put myself in that mindset." BUT "I really didn't have any parts" – Meaning that he vamps through the whole song.

The basic tracks were recorded live together in the studio including "95%" of the vocals, which would have made it more difficult to isolate the sounds.

The title track was produced & mixed solely by Tony Visconti & has a lot more life to it (& the sax mixed back to sound like DS was in the loo) but for the other Sigma tracks, after Visconti had followed Bowie's notes on what he wanted done, Bowie & Harry Maslin tweaked the results.

Recording Across The Universe was a way to flatter John Lennon & hook him in, but I've always wondered if including it wasn't a way to avoid possible copyright infringement for the "I heard the News today" quote.

Reading through lots of reviews over the last month, I'd never noticed that Young Americans opening chords are the same as Satellite of Love.

retropath2 says

25/07/2021 at 06:58

A superb essay; a bit like travel writing at its best, able to captivate, whether you have ever been there or not. Or even ever plan to. I have never heard YA, bar the singles, and feel that won't change as a result of the read, but I sure as hell enjoyed reading about it. Given there are a few other Bowie LPs I haven't heard, please keep writing.

For more comments and to join the conversation go to https://theafterword.co.uk/12-bowie-albums-in-12-months-young-americans/

Month 8

August 21st

Station To Station

When I started this Odyssey, this deep dive back into Bowie's back catalogue, 12 albums that I'd never heard before, at the back of my mind was the hope that somewhere I'd find some inspiration. Not for me you understand but for one of my musical heroes, Billy MacKenzie. I've mentioned this often enough so apologies but for those who aren't aware. From what I've read about Billy and the Associates they were very much inspired by Bowie but so far I'd only found scraps. I was left disappointed and disillusioned by *Young Americans* a lovely mid-80s yuppie coffee table style album. It's ok, jazzy and smooth, but it would sit comfortably alongside Sade's *Diamond Life* or The Style Council's *Café Bleu*. Great albums but not exactly what I was looking for. I must admit I was left a little flat almost to the point of giving up hope but thanks to some words of encouragement on this website I decided to carry on and give *Station To Station* a go. I'm so glad I did. I'm delighted to say it was a worthwhile experience. Finally, perhaps, (no pun intended), perhaps I have found the spark that ignited a young Alan Rankine and a young Billy MacKenzie to make music. Music that really had a massive effect on me and that I still listen to and love today.

I'm going to try and stick to the Bowie theme but I am going to ask you to indulge me a little, accept my artistic licence and understand that I might get a little bit carried away with this one but please bear with me. They're just my thoughts exactly as they popped into my head as I listened to *Station To Station* - and I have listened to it a lot and not just for the sake of doing this article but because it is a fantastic album. I hope I can give you a sense of why I feel it's that great and relevant over the rest of this piece.

So, on to the album. I found a *Rolling Stone* article and I'm going to pinch this quote from it.

"Critic Lester Bangs, an outspoken Bowie skeptic, wrote that the album "has a wail and throb that won't let up ... a beautiful, swelling, intensely romantic melancholy." Bowie, Bangs concluded, "has finally produced his (first) masterpiece."

I can't argue with that so onto the title track.

Station To Station. From the first few seconds of its industrial intro I was reminded of the first Associates album *The Affectionate Punch* and Logan Time, A, Transport To Central, all those wonderfully hypnotic, ethereal and enthralling songs. The first six minutes are a template for an electronic movement that exploded after punk. Vocally there are real comparisons to be made between Bowie and MacKenzie. I wish I knew the technical terms but in the lower register when the words are almost spoken it is uncannily similar. It's impossible not to imagine Rankine and MacKenzie in a bedroom in Dundee listening to this song and forming their own ideas on the theme. Was this the Associates "big bang" moment? I suspect so. But of course, this is David Bowie so he does return to David Quoie for the last four minutes along with some guitar work that wouldn't be out of place if used by The Darkness. A strong, exciting start.

Golden Years next. The hit. This is where I start to wonder if I'm hallucinating. I hear Club Country in the rhythms, the flow, the beat, when Bowie sings "Angel". I don't know. I just feel it. Maybe it was a subconscious influence on The Associates or maybe I just really want it to be there. But of course this is David Bowie and it's a Stevie Wonder inspired track that's one hell of a groove. What a song. One of those Bowie "hits" that you've heard too often but when you really hear it, man, it's wonderful.

Word On A Wing is a lovely song that takes me straight to some of the later solo Billy MacKenzie material, especially that found on the posthumously released Beyond The Sun. Strangely there was a review posted today on "The Affectionate Bunch" Facebook page which mentions *"Billy's brazen Bowie/Ferry infatuation"* and also this line which I'm having, *"THAT voice, sighing and smouldering and soaring to new heights of magnificent self obsession"*. That could account for Bowie's vocal on Word On A Wing too. But of course this is David Bowie and he takes the song off on a Jim Steinmanesque journey to its glorious conclusion. Dramatic and overblown but somehow just right in the way other attempts on other albums left me cold.

TVC 15 has fewer Associates references for me apart from the opening "Oh oh oh oh oh". I can't hear anything else really. But of course this is David Bowie and every album has had one that I can call my least favourite song on the album. The boogie woogie piano, the repetition of the title, it just sounds like a really 70s song.

Stay comes next. Wow! Where do I start? How do I unpick this? I'll start with what could be me the most out there reference point and this hit me from the first time I heard it. The part where Bowie sings an elongated "Stay" immediately put me in mind of the elongated "So" sung by Billy in Party Fears Two. Once I'd heard that, much like the Golden Years/Club Country mash up I can really hear a similarity in feel and vocal. Obviously, it's nothing like Party Fears Two but my fevered mind can't shake the feeling that it was an influence on parts of the song. There are other moments where Bowie's vocal can clearly be heard when Billy MacKenzie is toning down the operatic side of his voice. I would love to get my thoughts in front of Alan Rankine, maybe Facebook will allow that to happen. But of course this is David Bowie and he takes his *Young Americans* groove off into the stratosphere with Stay. It's a funky, dirty, gloriously driven song which Bowie sings perfectly. The outro is a crazy mix of Santana and Isley Brothers guitar. His best six minutes? Maybe. I love it.

Wild Is The Wind closes the album. A song I heard first sung by Billy on *Transmission Impossible*. I've since discovered there's probably more singers that haven't covered it than have, since it was used in the film of the same name in 1957. Nina Simone, George Michael, Bon Jovi, the list goes on. Billy's version will always be the definitive one for me. His control, his range, the moments he holds back and the moments he really soars is extraordinary. Of course, he would never have sung it had it not been for Bowie's version on *Station To Station* so for that one certainty alone *Station To Station* will have its place in my heart. But of course this is David Bowie and he just doesn't have that range vocally, he can't soar so he stretches and breaks a little but that gives his version a fragility that is quite moving. The fact that the band play like a wedding band behind him is something I can't figure out but it's Bowie and he does what he does and people love him for it. Right now, I love him for it too.

I once wrote.

"For some reason I don't quite understand Billy affects me more than any other pop star. Something about his ridiculous talent alongside his suffocating vulnerability and self doubt constantly draws me back."

To now find this album that in my mind appears to be a moment, the conception, the beginning of what became The Associates and put me inside the heads of Billy MacKenzie and Alan Rankine in 1977 is quite something. Maybe after seven months of searching like an archaeologist finding a pot from the local store and desperately trying to age it at 10,000 years, I'm hearing something that isn't there but in the spirit of these posts I'm putting it out there for dissection by my peers. But of course this David Bowie his imagination, his sense of drama, his refusal to conform, need to take risks and his invention has frustrated, confused and delighted me in equal measure over those seven months. Even on this album there is some really unusual musical weirdness that made me scratch my head. It's a great album and one I'll definitely listen to again. I'm looking forward to the *Berlin Trilogy* with renewed enthusiasm for what I'll find next. *Station To Station* will take its place in my collection. A mosquito set in amber from which the DNA of a band and singer that affect me like no other was extracted to create something remarkably similar while remaining thrillingly different.

Comments From The Afterword

noisecandy says

21/08/2021 at 11:54

'A great review. Station to Station is one of my favourite Bowie albums. Golden Year' slightly borrows the riff from The Drifters 'On Broadway'. Bowie also considered offering this track to Elvis Presley but this never materialised. He also stated that he'd been approached by an RCA executive with a view to producing and writing songs for Elvis. Six months later Elvis was dead. A lost opportunity leaving Bowie heartbroken.

Diddley Farquar says

21/08/2021 at 12:59

One of my favourite albums. Been listening to it for over 40 years. Still sounds fresh and bright. The best Bowie period in my view: 76-80. The best musicians he worked with. A hint of what post punk could be, how you could make imaginative guitar rock without the old blues rock tropes. Also the funk element which many would take up, here now fully integrated. Great to read this take on it.

Vincent says

22/08/2021 at 16:59

These are the correct answers. I'd push the significant year range by one to 1975 – "five years" as it were. Though I love the hippie/ hard rock, then glam Bowie, the albums I come back to are "Young Americans" to "Lodger", and "STS" noses it for my favourite. I grudgingly accept that "Scary Monsters" might be better than I thought. All done whilst producing THAT corpus of albums and singles over a decade (better than The Beatles to me), he managed to also redefine the nature of the rock concert in a few world tours (or at least half-inch a gallimaufry of ideas and integrate them into a more accomplished sense of performance), act in a few films, have a hearty and mind-bending habit, clean up with iggy Pop in Berlin (what can one say?), remain well-read, and curated the cultural world of his more bookish and arty fans. As I've said before, Bowie was one of the hip older brothers who shaped a generation's culture and taste beyond the music. And he didn't fly in a plane, either. This is better than 2 weeks with "Sexy Sadie" and a week in bed for peace. The Associates connection is well-made (another of us provincials holding onto Bowie to point the way out), and Billy Mackenzie's "Secret Life of Arabia" is also excellent:

Moose the Mooche says

21/08/2021 at 18:02

My theory is that there are elements of STS in all of his good albums afterwards, especially the title track, and as such it is his most important album apart from Hunky Dory regardless of whether it's his best.

Blue Boy says

23/08/2021 at 20:04

Another one here for whom Station to Station is not just Bowie's finest hour, but one of the high points of all pop music. And it has aged incredibly well- glad you enjoyed it Dave and that it prompted such a great post.

Junior Wells says

24/08/2021 at 11:00

My one beef is Dave's dismissal of TVC 15. It's an excellent track, really swings and fits wonderfully.

Timbar says

26/08/2021 at 18:48

"Fame" had finally given Bowie a number one US single & Station to Station backed up that success – top 3 album, his best US chart performance until "The Next Day" Bowie sings in a fairly comfortable range without many "Bowie inflections" which helped it appeal to a mainstream audience & made the songs ideal for performing live ("I'm just doing this tour for the money. I never earned any money before, but this time I'm going to make some. I think I deserve it, don't you?) Using the DAM (Davis, Alomar, Murray) rhythm section that would stay with him for the rest of the decade, they worked up the backing tracks first & then added solos, lyrics & vocals. Harry Maslin said that Golden Years was "cut and finished very fast" but "the rest of the album took forever". It does seem that lots of time was spent tinkering (not helped by Bowie's prestigious cocaine use) and adding lots of overdubs. For all of the time spent, Station to Station has a very clear, uncluttered sound – which is one of the reasons that it has aged so well – the dance around the drums at the end of "Wild is the Wind" still sounds fantastic. Bowie later said that he wanted to do a dead mix "I gave in and added that extra commercial touch. I wish I hadn't". However, it was that commercial success that gave him the freedom to move on...

For more comments and to join the conversation go to https://theafterword.co.uk/12-bowie-albums-in-12-months-station-to-station/

Month 9

September 25th

Low

Month 9 of 12 Bowie Albums in 12 Months. Bloody hell, how did that happen? Three quarters of the way through this dive into Bowie having never listened to one of his albums before. After the high of *Station To Station* the next album *Low* had something to live up to. I try to limit my research as I want to come to these albums as fresh as possible. Coming to this knowing he was off the drugs, living in Berlin and experimenting musically was encouraging yet slightly worrying at the same time. What would clean arty Bowie cone up with? Let's see, or hear, whatever.

It starts with **Speed Of Life** an instrumental, not the last as I would discover later but with all the build up it's a pretty basic straight up rock 'n' roll number that does include some Human League style keyboards. I found myself making up lyrics that Mick Jagger might have sung as it reminded me of 80s Rolling Stones in the style of Undercover Of The Night.

You done me young you won't do that twice cos,

I'm moving on at the speed of life.

I won't be coming round in the dead of night cos,

I'm moving on at the speed of life

Etcetera. You get the point. It's ok, but as an opener? I know by now it's Bowie so I shouldn't be surprised.

Next up is **Breaking Glass** which I assume Nick Lowe loved the sound of. Not for the first time it reminds me of The White Stripes. Meg's drumming remains pretty rudimentary. Again, there's some random keyboard thrown in and it finishes pretty abruptly. It's OK.

What In The World takes me back to *Station To Station* and The Associates comparisons again. The mix of keyboards and guitar works really well and it's a great noise. I like it.

The hit next. **Sound and Vision**. From nowhere it's one of those great Bowie grooves. The band drive it on and I'm reminded of that clip of Stevie Wonder doing Superstition on *Sesame Street* with the coolest band you've ever seen. Of course it was a hit. It's another of those ubiquitous Bowie songs that when you really hear it, wow. I suspect somewhere the band is still playing that groove it's so entrenched. I love it.

Always Crashing In The Same Car is a really cool song. I can't escape the feeling that it's a little bit Steely Dan but a slightly rougher version, less polished. The guitar in this is perfect for the kind of easy flow of the song. Whisky In The Jar-like in parts. Following the slightly odd opening this is a strong run of songs.

Be My Wife is Chas and Dave meets Van Halen meets The Stranglers. That's it. I've nothing else to say about it.

Typical Bowie fare so far. Eclectic, interesting but no real consistent style. That's fine, this is David Bowie he's earned the right to do whatever he wants. Now he does exactly that with five almost entirely instrumental tracks. Each one clearly experimental, exploring new ideas and sounds. As always, I'll tell you what I hear, here goes.

A New Career In A New Town starts like Blue Monday then becomes Madness doing The Return Of The Los Palmas 7 with plenty of Spaghetti Western harmonica.

Warszawa is more Joy Division than New Order mixed with Sting's Russians

Art Decade instantly makes me think of Japan. It's another track that in my head I sing in my best David Sylvian voice.

Art Decade..... (long pause here)

Is it real or an illusion?......(another long pause)

Art Decade.....

Thankfully for us all I can leave **Weeping Wall** be as an instrumental. My first thought was *Tubular Bells* (side 1 obviously). Then maybe because my Sylvian antenna had been agitated from the depths of my memory, I added Sakamoto. I had to go and rediscover *Forbidden Colours* and of course to complete the circle, *Merry Christmas Mr Lawrence*. This will be the point at which, Timbar, Tigger or Gary will regail stories of the links. It's what I've enjoyed most about these threads. I hear something familiar and an expert comes along to fill the gaps.

Finally **Subterraneans** in which you can imagine David Attenborough breathily expressing wonder at some creature just discovered at the bottom of the Atlantic. Musically I can imagine Midge Ure belting out "*Subterraneaaaaans*". It could on the other hand be one of Mark Hollis' more esoteric compositions. Whatever it is, its a bit lovely with its Gregorian chant / Kenny G sax to close.

So there it is *Low*. It's a grower, it's eclectic, it's Bowie. I have this vision of the recording studio with all these old guitar engineers tripping over wires and extension cables muttering about bloody keyboards while scratching their heads at the noises being called “music". Overall for me while I really like it I am left a little frustrated. Why Dave? Well imagine he’d gone all in on the electronica, the ambience, the Neu!? His influence from what he’d heard in Germany is clear but he’s only really committed in parts. It’s importance to the period that followed is clear. That period from 1979 to 1984 that to me is the most exciting, inventive, creative since Chuck Berry picked up his guitar, can be traced right back to this along with Kraftwerk I’m sure. If he’d really gone for it in 1976/77 *Low* could have been so ahead of it's time, such a defining work that it could have been discussed in almost Ark of the Covenant terms. After the clear *Station To Station* / The Associates link it will be interesting for me now to find definite references from those early 80s pioneers back to *Low* or at least the parts where he goes all in. Finally I think this album will take me on a Japan/Sylvian journey that I’ve been meaning to take for a long time.

Comments From The Afterword

Moose the Mooche says

25/09/2021 at 10:25

The great thing about your pieces Dave is that while I know what other people are going to say on these threads – in some cases almost word-for-word – I never know what you’re going to say. You’ve made connections and comparisons that would never occur to us old lightning-flashers (steady).

Black Celebration says

25/09/2021 at 11:51

Low has been in my life for a very long time and I come back to it pretty regularly. The instrumentals are what makes the album astonishing and a reissue also gives us All Saints, which fits in nicely. I'm not sure if I can describe those tracks and do them justice. There's just such a lot going on and so many noises and patterns that develop. And then on side 1 there's Be My Wife, which could be in a cheesy Tommy Steele film – and of course Bowie being a pop genius with Sound & Vision. It's a good square meal of an album. Thanks for writing about it because I'll be putting it on again soon. I love this record.

Moose the Mooche says

25/09/2021 at 14:16

I think the minimalism on the first side of Low is very clever. Bowie's vocals on "Heroes" are incredible. The latter is a more satisfying album but I've just got to admire the well-I-bet-you-didn't-see-THIS-coming chutzpah of Low. And it has Sound and Vision on it, which is beyond magnificent.

I've got Charles Shaar Murray's full-page review of Low from the NME and while he's impressed, he basically gets annoyed with Bowie for being so negative. These are desperate times and you need to give us hope, CSM says: I think it's pretty odd asking that from Bowie of all people, who had been mining the dark stuff fairly regularly since We are Hungry Men and the like. Ask Bowie to cheer up and you get Dancing in the Street, so think on.

Tiggerlion says

25/09/2021 at 17:57

Low is a perfect encapsulation of depression. Its soundscape is heavily compressed and difficult to make out individual instruments, almost painful to listen to. There are few words, just over 200 for the whole album, the least on any Bowie album, and unrelentingly miserable: "Don't look at the carpet, I've drawn something awful on it", "Blue, blue, electric blue, is the colour of my room where I will sit, waiting for the gift of sound and vision", "Sometimes you get so lonely, sometimes you get nowhere", "Something deep inside of me, yearning deep inside of me, talking through the gloom". These words are the voice of experience. CSM suffered with depression himself and would have known this.

Low was recorded in 1976 and released in January 1977 before The Human League was formed. It lit a flame that exploded in New Wave and the New Romantics. It inspired synth-pop and the likes of Joy Division and resonates through most Electronica even today. It is a musical Ark of the Covenant. To my ears, it still sounds ahead of its time. Great review, Dave, yet again. I think you are going to enjoy all of the last three.

For more comments and to join the conversation go to *https://theafterword.co.uk/12-bowie-albums-in-12-months-low/*

Month 10

October 23rd

"Heroes"

Arriving at month 10 I really feel like I'm in a peak Bowie phase. His delve into experimental electronica is proving to be my favourite period. I've heard much about the Berlin Trilogy and while geographically it may be a Trilogy, musically I'm getting the sense that it really started with *Station To Station* which would make it a quadrilogy? The Associates theme looms large and as they are one of the most important bands of my life, this 12 month project has really come to life and ***"Heroes"*** hasn't let me down. Just to shake things up a bit there'll be no references to other bands that I hear in this music. I'll try and keep to a pure review format because I think I've exhausted those references and I want to avoid too much repetition. I've done a bit of reading as always and my favourite line so far is this.

The album was recorded sporadically from July to August 1977. The majority of the tracks were composed on the spot in the studio, the lyrics not being written until Bowie stood in front of the microphone.

It's impressive if true because what comes next is just a little bit special.

Beauty and the Beast starts with a bit of improv piano and drums then drops in a wah wah noise that would wake the dead. He's got your attention already. Bowie then seemingly, finally completely in control of his vocals takes us through a power house of a song with ghostly "whooo's" and edge of his range "my, mys" with female backing to lift it another level. There's the thought that this could have been one of those tracks that just never gets going on previous albums but here it just keeps coming. Guitars mixed with keyboards and a beat that doesn't let go. It's some opener.

Joe The Lion is more of the same, if more guitar lead. It grabs you and just keeps going. Bowie telling a story that may have made sense in his head but has anyone ever deciphered these lyrics?

Joe the lion went to the bar

A couple of drinks on the house and he was

A fortune teller he said nail me to my car

And I'll tell you who you are

I imagine it's great live song.

Now I don't suppose I'll come up with anything new about "**Heroes"**. I will say hearing it in among this collection has given it new context for me. Much loved by television sporting montage makers its ubiquity has dulled its greatness but hearing it here has given it new life. Such a simple yet clever song. Straight off with a basic backing beat accompanied by long single keyboard notes that stretch out endlessly but hypnotically. Is this *the* blueprint for my early 80s heroes? I can only imagine being 15 or 16 hearing this and thinking "that's what I want to do". This is Bowie's greatest vocal achievement as the music just keeps going without crescendo; that all comes from the vocal, another part of the song copied by many a young vocalist. Right now, it's my favourite Bowie song. I really need a word with 12-year old me who probably dismissed it. It's perfect.

This being Bowie of course he deflates my balloon of wonder a little with **Sons of the Silent Age**. Maybe because it follows Heroes but its stage-Bowie rearing his head again with the sax and the harmonies just not working for me. Expectations raised it's perhaps not surprising but onwards we go.

Blackout raises the bar again, another song that drives along with a mix of guitar and keyboard that finishes side one nicely. I've used "nicely" in a Bowie review, oh dear. On to side two where the fun really starts.

The title **V-2 Schneider** is so intriguing that I have to look it up. My thoughts that it referred to version two of Bo Duke was clearly wide of the mark. It's Florian Schneider from Kraftwerk meets a V-2 rocket. Of course it is. Either way it's a gloriously bonkers almost instrumental track that mixes just about everything that they had in the studio that made a sound. The almost lost-in-the-mix vocal repetition of the title gives it an otherworldly feel among the recognisable sounds. It's all just a delicious pick and mix for your ears.

How to describe **Sense Of Doubt**? Well clearly it's another electronic piece supplemented by piano that sounds like the noise I used to make on my Aunt's piano when I was 9 and fascinated by the lower register keys. However, what I really hear is one of those dramatic seascapes in sonic form, dark and foreboding. A mix of colour and form and impending doom. I found a painting, "The Ninth Wave" by Ivan Aivazovsky which illustrates it perfectly. The song and the painting are both glorious.

It segues seamlessly into **Moss Garden** which is soothing, calming and the sort of thing you'd want to meditate to. I'm going with a Japanese feel although it could equally be Indian. A biwa perhaps or shamisen or sitar over an ambient, electronic backing. It's a haunting, whisper of a track that takes you into a Garden of Eden of sound. Ommmm.

Neuköln on the other hand is bleak and industrial. Church-like organ playing out a scene from a night time red light area full of suspicious characters and cheap thrills and danger on every corner. It's so atmospheric, and engaging. It's the end to a quite extraordinary run of instrumentals.

The album ends on a song I'm very familiar with. **The Secret Life Of Arabia** is an upbeat ahead of its time piece of pop that doesn't quite fit with anything else on the album but that doesn't matter. Somehow it works, Bowie's vocal is bang on it again to finish off a quite remarkable album.

So I quite like *"Heroes"* then. I checked the charts for 1977 and it's that period between ABBA and The Sex Pistols in amongst Rod Stewart and The Stranglers and here was Bowie ignoring all that and doing his own thing. Continuing to lay down the template for what was to come when electronic music really exploded. I came into this project as a cynic who needed convincing. There were snippets of what others heard but it never completely clicked with me. Then came the crashing disappointment of *Young Americans*. Since then for me to deny what followed through *Station to Station, Low* and now *"Heroes"*, when I've spent the last few years telling anyone who'd listen how the early 80s were the pinnacle of popular music, would render these reviews completely worthless. I cannot deny their brilliance and importance in the unimportant world of popular music. I will seek out vinyl copies of these three albums. Who knows about *Lodger* and *Scary Monsters*? We'll see. Not to listen to necessarily but to help tell the story of the rest of my collection from 1980 onwards. Like any collector my prized artefacts will remain so but owning these records will help define them, tell their story, and as I've said before, let me get inside the heads of my heroes as their creative spark was ignited by a man who would clearly have been a hero of theirs.

We could steal time just for one day,

We can be heroes for ever and ever.

What d'you say?

Comments From The Afterword

Black Type says

23/10/2021 at 18:05

The featured instrument on Moss Garden is a Japanese koto, which gives it the distinctive Far Eastern vibe. The Dame was a noted Japanophile, but certainly no Weeaboo.

GCU Grey Area says

23/10/2021 at 20:00

Fripp's sustained guitar on 'Heroes' was done 'old school', I think, by feedback from his guitar amp in the studio. Notes were changed by a combo of string bends, and moving to/away from the amp, with duct tape on the floor as a guide. He seems to do the song nowadays with a Fernades sustainer pickup on his guitar, as does Steve Hackett on his Les Paul-types.

Moose the Mooche says

23/10/2021 at 20:10

Apart from Sgt Pepper, Exile OMS and SMiLE, is the making of any album as mythologised as this one? And it's funny that it's become, apart maybe from Hunky, his most celebrated album when it died on its arse on release.

Lodestone of Wrongness says

23/10/2021 at 21:01

"Heroes was a commercial success, peaking at number 3 on the UK Albums Chart and number 35 on the US Billboard Top LPs & Tape chart. It was the best-received work of the Berlin Trilogy on release, with NME and Melody Maker naming it Album of the Year." Even me, a well-known and much admired (?) Bowie sceptic, immediately fell in love with Heroes. Dying on its arse it did not do

slotbadger says

24/10/2021 at 12:15

This is the album for me, I so taken by it I actually moved to Berlin and would walk around Neukolln late at night listening to it on my headphones (dodging the hordes of other "sensitive" British blokes wandering around the streets doing exactly the same thing)

Sense of Doubt is walking up Karl Marx Allee at sunrise on a winter mornings, flanked by peeling old Soviet housing blocks and massive, imposing Brutalist buildings.

Beauty And The Beast is wandering on a busy night down Ku'damm. Joe The Lion ditto, through Kreuzberg

Heroes itself is wonderful when listened to walking north east of Potsdamerplatz, past Hansa Studios itself

NigelT says

28/10/2021 at 13:08

I hadn't heard the album in donkey's years, so I dug out my old 70s vinyl copy today. To be honest, I never really liked this or Low all that much back in the day – my memory was of some great tracks, but some rather tedious instrumental stuff. I actually have revised my opinion now – I guess my 70 something self has got a little more open minded than my 20 something counterpart, which I find surprising! So, I followed it up with Low and Lodger (which I always did like) and had a brilliant afternoon!

duco01 says

09/11/2021 at 11:42

1. "Heroes" always used to be my favourite Bowie album, but I think that Low has just about overtaken it now. It's a close call, though. They're both brilliant, and the Berlin period has always been my No.1 Bowie era.

2. Has anyone on this thread mentioned the fact that "Heroes" (the album and the song) must always be written in inverted commas? (Welch, Chris (1999). "David Bowie: Changes, 1970–1980". p. 116. The use of quotation marks around the title meant that Bowie felt there was something ironic about being a rock 'n' roll hero to his fans, while he kept his own emotional life as far distant and remote and private as possible.)

3. I like that bit in Blackout where Bowie cries "I'm under Japanese influence and my honour's at stake!"

4. I love Joe the Lion. It must be, technically, a very difficult song to sing.

5. The only track I've never cared for is "The Secret Life of Arabia". I'm rather surprised by how popular it is among Afterworders.

For more comments and to join the conversation go to https://theafterword.co.uk/12-bowie-albums-in-12-months-heroes/

Month 11

November 25th

Lodger

Believe it or not I'm at month 11, the penultimate look into 12 David Bowie albums having never heard one before. I've arrived at *Lodger* the third of the much vaunted *Berlin Trilogy* despite there being a whole two years between *"Heroes"* and *Lodger*. (Did Bowie run for cover during punk?) There's Bowie prostrate on the ground on the album cover like an extra from *Silent Witness* and just one track I recognise. Can it follow the recent high watermark of the real trilogy (regardless of where they were made) of *Station To Station*, *Low* and *Heroes*? Does *Lodger* make it a foursome? Well no it doesn't, it's very different. Gone are the ambient, electronic sweeps of sound and glory replaced by an edgy, angular post punk sound right in the middle of the post punk era. This is not Bowie looking to the future or the past, this is Bowie slap bang in the middle of where it's at. The first listen brought many familiar sounds from the era popping round my brain. So, much like my reimagining of *Aladdin Sane* as a 1973 episode of Top Of The Pops this review will take the form of a reimagined late night 1979 radio show. It could be Peel, it could be Jensen, it could be Peebles or even Partridge if you'd prefer. There will be a look back, the latest releases, an import and of course a session from the latest thing. There may even be "two more from them later". Indulge me again as I ask you to gather round your medium wave radio tuned to Radio Dave in 1979 and enjoy the show. (It might help if you read the italics in the voice of your favourite late night DJ, sardonic Liverpudlian, excitable Canadian etc.)

"Well tonight's programme is a collection of the latest sounds from what I'm calling "Post Punk". You'll hear some of the best upcoming and unsigned bands out there. Starting tonight with a young band from Glasgow recently formed and hoping to have an album released soon. This is Orange Juice with **Fantastic Voyage***."*

There's something in the drum and bass backing and Bowie's vocal that puts me in mind of Edwyn and co that places this firmly on their first album *You Can't Hide Your Love Forever*. 1979 is a little early but it's what I hear. It's a great opener, melodic and dreamy and perfect post punk fodder for the cool kids who've started wearing their now trendy dad's clothes.

"Next tonight is the first from our session with Adam and The Ants. Front man Stuart Goddard was so inspired by The Sex Pistols when his band Bazooka Joe headlined the Pistols first live gig he completely changed his look, name and sound. They're now earning rave reviews for their energy and live performances touring wth Siouxsie and the Banshees. This is **African Night Flight***."*

The rhythms and overall sound of African Night Flight instantly put me in mind of Adam and The Ants as a sort of hybrid of the punk version and the hit making 80's monster they became. It would definitely fit on *Dirk Wears White Sox* as easily as *Kings Of The Wild Frontier*. Trust me this is a huge compliment from someone who believes Adam Ant to be one of *the* great pop stars however fleetingly his star shone. It's a really brilliant song showing Bowie at his most creative even managing to predate Stormzy by 40 years with his intense rapped lyrical interlude.

"That's Adam and The Ants, two more from them later.. Next a look back to a band from the early 70s who's hits came just a

couple of years ago and who some might describe as proto punk but this song fits with tonight's show. It's The Modern Lovers with **Move On***."*

Ok I've stretched the theme a bit here but I can't shake the feeling that I'm listening to Roadrunner the driving almost galloping rhythm is very similar. It also brings to mind the greatest TV theme ever The Flashing Blade. Again, these are complimentary comparisons for another brilliantly upbeat song.

"That was Move On which we must do here on Radio Dave to our next tune from a rag tag bunch of London squatters who will invite you on stage to join them if you attend one of their live performances. It's Thompson Twins with **Yassassin** *which is Turkish for long live apparently."*

Now before you start cursing me and asking how I'm comparing Bowie with the We Are Detective hitmakers, please wait. If you suffered my Thompson Twins reappraisal earlier this year, you'll know that early Thompson Twins were very different to the big haired chart botherers they became. In 1979 they had two Peel sessions and were quite the "thing". I would stake my Doctor Doctor picture disc on the fact that by the time they released their first album *A Product of...* in 1981 Tom Bailey had listened to *Lodger* a lot. Yassassin is really wonderful and evocative and hypnotic and I love it.

"Back from our trip to the bazaars and souks of Turkey we are off to the roundabouts and trading estates of Swindon the home of our next band. On their third album and making plans for more it's XTC and **Red Sails***."*

From the opening guitar to the vocal I immediately thought of Andy Partridge. The delivery of the lyric, the tune, it all screamed XTC. I had to do some digging and there it was in 1979 on *Drums and Wires* full of jangle, edge and that Partridge vocal. Another stormer of a tune. There is no let up with *Lodger* as side one closes.

"That was XTC and you're listening to Radio Dave and only here can you go from Turkey to Swindon to New York in search of the best new post punk sounds. Here is a band from New York with an import only release. They're now working with Brian Eno which you can hear loud and clear on this track it's Talking Heads with **DJ***."*

Full disclosure here. I heard Talking Heads musically several times on *Lodger* and it was only when I was doing a little reading on the album and Talking Heads that I realised just how much cross pollination was going on. My ears can be trusted sometimes. It turns out Bowie is deliberately mimicking David Byrne. I'm hoping someone will fill in the back story in more detail. It's a song that lifts *Lodger* to another level. It's post punk plus. It has energy, drive and I'm astonished it only reached number 29 when released as a single in the UK.

"Well that's one take on being a DJ. If I am what I play then tonight I'm a portal to the best new music out there like this next song. Another young Scottish band earning great reviews for their live shows. They'll be joining us soon for a session. Can they transfer that live sound onto their recorded material? Let's see. It's Simple Minds with **Look Back In Anger***."*

I must admit when I first heard Look Back In Anger I was drawn in by the sheer energy of it and placed it around *Once Upon A Time* Simple Minds. However once I'd given their 1979 album *Life In A Day* a listen there it was. No one was copying anyone here I guess in 1979 these were the sounds and technology available to bands and producers. In a tough field Look Back In Anger could be my favourite. *Lodger* just keeps coming. No ambient relaxation moments here..

"There's Simple Minds bringing that energy right into your room through your speakers. We're staying North of the border for two lads from Dundee hoping that this track will get them noticed. A copy arrived in the post today, very cheeky. I think it will do the trick though. This is the currently unsigned Associates with **Boys Keep Swinging**.*"*

As you probably know by now finding these connections to The Associates and getting inside the minds of the young Billy and Alan has been one of the highlights of this whole project. They put out a version of Boys Keep Swinging without permission just six weeks after the release of *Lodger* and it did indeed get them noticed. How important was it? Would they have caught a break without it? We'll never know but as part of The Associates story it's absolutely vital. Of course, I love it although much like Wild Is The Wind it's hard for me to not hear Billy's voice. Bowie's version is dynamic and edgy with a real punch. I can absolutely understand why The Associates chose it.

"That's The Associates there proving that mimicry is indeed the greatest form of flattery as someone once said. Some brilliant records tonight proving that we are entering a golden period for music. We're finishing tonight with two more from our session band Adam and The Ants. **Repetition** *and* **Red Money**. *I'm off for a pint and pie and I'll see you tomorrow If you fancy it. Over to you Adam."*

Unless I'm really losing the plot with this you can't help but feel the Ant vibe in these last two tracks. Both utterly brilliant. I really hope that the Adam and The Ants comparisons don't offend any hardcore Bowie fans. None of these are done with anything but affection. *Lodger* was one of those albums that from the first listen to the last (probably twenty or so) it was like an explosion of familiar sounds from a time when I was just starting to pay attention to a musical world outside of ABBA and The Wombles. 1979 marked the start of the peak musical period of my life and it feels like the world had probably caught up with Bowie but looking at album and single chart positions his core audience were still with him. It's interesting how Bowie's career and some of the bands I reference took similar paths through the next few years. Arty post punk posers through to glossy video making unit shifting posers. Anyway, for me this is a really strong album and more consistent than many before. There are no weak links and I'm left wondering what might have happened if my older brother had brought this home instead of the latest release from The Police or The Jam. It really doesn't fit with the previous three albums.

As a footnote, during some research I found out that Gary Numan's success in 1979 upset Bowie and many of his fans which surprises me; even though Are Friends Electric would have been a natural successor to *"Heroes"* it feels like Bowie had moved on and Numan just took huge influence from Bowie's electronic experimentation. Bowie could have gone all out electronic in 1979 but perhaps he misread the room or just decided that he'd done that and as previously just wanted to try something different.

Lodger would fit perfectly in any post punk / new wave collection and it's one I'll return to. That's four belters in a row which just leaves me with *Scary Monsters*. An early sneaky look at the track listing tells me already its one to look forward to.

Comments From The Afterword

dai says

25/11/2021 at 21:54

Nice piece. I think the trilogy thing is a bit contrived. It's an Eno period rather than a Berlin one. Lodger was recorded in Switzerland mostly, but also in New York. It also has much less in common with the other two which are really a similar pair.

I like it a fair amount, but don't love it. Might just about sneak into my top 10 or 12 Bowie albums on a good day. I love Boys Keep Swinging which was the first Bowie record I bought at the time of release (although probably discounted in Woolworths' ex chart bin). Fantastic Voyage is superb (also the B side of that single), but rest of side 1 doesn't do an awful lot for me. Side 2 may be better, first 3 tracks up there with anything he was doing in that period.

Look forward to the Scary next one!

Tiggerlion says

26/11/2021 at 07:35

Punk only really existed 76/77 when we got Low and "Heroes" plus The Idiot and Lust For Life, not to mention a tour as Iggy Pop's keyboard player. Bowie had a good Punk.

I'm really fond of this album and listen to it a lot. It gave birth to the New Romantics who first gathered at Bowie/Roxy nights to pose to their records. I see DJ as autobiography; David Jones, a man reduced to playing his records at home while his girlfriend is out dancing.

fentonsteve says

26/11/2021 at 11:23

I love Post-Punk as a genre, but this is my least-favourite of the Berlin quadrilogy (which starts with STS). Possibly because it sounds less like Bowie going it alone and more like others. I'll have to go and have another listen now.

Moose the Mooche says

26/11/2021 at 14:47

I've a lot of affection for this, partly as it was the first Bowie album I heard all the way through. In early 1981 it already seemed obscure and forgotten and nothing to do with anything, not even the two Bowie songs I was familiar with (A2A and Fashion).

What a range of music to be exposed to at the age of (eeeek!) seven. Is this the same bloke as the one in the clown costume on the orange beach on the telly? He's clearly a nutter. I like him!

Diddley Farquar says

26/11/2021 at 15:00

I think Lodger got known as the one that was not quite as good as the other Berlin trilogy albums. Critics expected one innovative masterpiece after another. In those days a lot was expected of the more acclaimed acts. One year you are it, the next you are finished. They got it wrong here I reckon. I think these songs are more fully formed than many on Heroes and Low. Bowie is current here with the post punk feel and the sense of world influences. The singing is among his best, the band is great. The critics may have wanted a trilogy to sound more like a trilogy (though it wasn't a trilogy) and felt let down. Take it as a bunch of great tunes and performances and it's a blast. Scary Monsters is a kind of continuation but Lodger is more consistent probably. Lodger doesn't have an Ashes To Ashes though, which is an all time high

Moose the Mooche says

26/11/2021 at 21:04

Getting some hardcore black American funkateers to play Neu! is quite funny. And it works. Woody would have played that motorik beat as the Glitter Band which would just have been silly. Michael Ronson doing Michael Rother after the example of his own work on Width of a Circle would have been quite cool though but.

fatima Xberg says

27/11/2021 at 11:29

"Lodger" is indeed very playful and tongue in cheek. There was a piece in Melody Maker at the time of the album's release where Bowie explained the "concepts" behind each track. For example, "Move On" is "All The Young Dudes" backwards (apparently), and three songs have the same identical chords. "Repetition" was an exercise of the musicians playing instruments they are not familiar with (Dave: "There was real enthusiasm suddenly…").

For more comments and to join the conversation go to https://theafterword.co.uk/12-bowie-albums-in-12-months-lodger/

Month 12

December 18th

Scary Monsters and Super Creeps

While the rest of you have been compiling your best of 2021 and trying to avoid Last Christmas by Wham I've been listening to *Scary Monsters (and Super Creeps)*. My final Bowie album of the year.

Released in September 1980 just as many of his musical disciples were hitting their stride. Adam and The Ants were about to go full dressing up box with *Kings of the Wild Frontier*, The Associates had just released *The Affectionate Punch*, Visage were readying their eponymous album for release (more on them later) while Japan would release *Gentlemen Take Polaroids* in November 1980. All these bands and more had listened and watched and taken influence musically and visually, from Bowie and now here they were releasing albums alongside him. What would Bowie come up with? His 12th album in under 10 years, 10 years of wildly varying styles and sounds that delighted, inspired, baffled and frustrated the music buying public in equal measure, now competing with those he influenced.

There was a real hope that I could sign off on a 100% stone cold classic, where all the stars aligned and I could declare myself fully indoctrinated into the David Bowie fanclub. So with a mixture of excitement, trepidation and some relief that my self imposed Bowiethon was coming to an end, I dropped the needle (pressed play on Spotify), sat back in my favourite armchair (the driver's seat of my car on my journey to work) and once again immersed myself in a Bowie album (listened when I could between work and life).

The cover image was instantly recognisable and the track listing favourable, four songs I knew, two of which were massively popular. This would be blast.

It's No Game (No. 1) kicks off with a sound effects intro that has hints of Depeche Mode and a 1,2,3,4 gear change into some spoken Japanese words that instantly put me in mind of the spoken French in Visage's Fade To Grey. Then some guitar I recognise as Robert Fripp (get me) and then it's all about Bowie's vocal histrionics which take him from a Dave Grohl scream to the very edge of his range and back again. It's a heady, exhilarating start as Fripp's guitar takes centre stage in between all the vocal shenanigans.

Up The Hill Backwards next. Imagine a song that starts with Dave Edmund's Queen Of Hearts, Buddy Holly's Not Fade Away and Bow Wow Wow's I Want Candy all mixed up to make the intro then drops into a rather monotone lyrical delivery over a marching drum sound reminiscent of Arcade Fire before switching back again to the mix of the intro. Yep, that's Up The Hill Backwards. Not one of my favourites and a surprising choice for a single but very, very Bowie.

Scary Monsters (and Super Creeps) follows and Bowie's lyrical acrobatics are at the fore again and it reminds me of The Psychedelic Furs Pretty In Pink in sound and vocal. Maybe a hint of Human League's Sound Of The Crowd in the outro. There's also the first flash of something in the whole feel of the song that increases over the next couple of tracks. We've arrived at the sound of the Blitz Kids.

Ashes To Ashes is so familiar to everyone there's little I can say that can possibly bring anything new. It's a remarkable song and it had that video that was so visually stunning and included an appearance by Steve Strange. One of those "I remember when I first saw it" moments. How could it not be an influence? Hold on to your fancy hats here Bowie lovers but it's obvious how much Bowie's look and sound influenced the already formed Spandau Ballet and Duran Duran. Listen to John Taylor's bass on Save A Prayer and the bass on Ashes To Ashes. Then of course the look and style of what became known as the New Romantics.

Fashion follows and it's such a new romantic anthem. Whenever clips are shown of The Blitz or The Rum Runner in one of the endless 80s music documentaries the chances are the kids are dancing to Fashion. Dressed in tablecloths, bin bags and leather with striking hair and make up moving jerkily to the beat. Bowie and Roxy Music nights defined that era and spawned loads of bands that are oft derided by the same people who cite Bowie as a genius. They were his creation. Without him they would have just played guitars wearing jeans and t shirts. Fashion is an absolute tune by the way. It is, however, the last of the New Romantic Genesis Trilogy. Maybe Bowie was bored of influencing a generation but there is no doubt in my mind that he had. What does surprise me is the overlap in 1980. I had it fixed in my head for some reason that Visage, Spandau Ballet and Duran Duran had been created and followed this version of Bowie entirely. Visage and Spandau released their first hits in 1980 and Duran Duran early in 1981. A really quick turn around but the influence is too obvious to ignore. Either way the whole melting pot was an incredibly exciting period for pop music and as I've said. It's all down to Bowie.

Teenage Wildlife follows and to my ears is a middle of the road song that could have come from the mid-seventies or the mid-eighties. Bowie's ever more desperate attempts to lift it with ever more, vocal cartwheels and some hair guitar solos fail to lift it for me. Sorry.

Scream Like A Baby is another flat song that you can't believe is from the same album as Fashion. Theatrical Bowie comes up from the footlights again before the Daleks join in for a *Dr Who* interlude. I'm lost. You tell me what I'm supposed to hear here.

Kingdom Come is a funny little song. I've mentioned a few times how much Dr Robert from The Blow Monkeys must have been influenced by Bowie's vocals. This actually sounds like Bowie is trying to mimic Dr Robert (I realise this is an analogy rendered impossible by time) such is the exaggerated vibrato in his vocal. It's lifted by Fripp's guitar and some interesting backing vocals but for me fails to scale the earlier heights.

Because You're Young starts like a scene from *Scooby Doo* as Scooby and Shaggy try to avoid this week's monster. It then veers off into some Stranglers keyboards and Bowie trying to build some drama. It has a decent chorus and I like the idea of Bowie going full Tarzan at the end but again, for me, it just doesn't match the earlier part of the album.

It's No Game (No.2) closes the album. It's clear there was something profound going on in comparison to (No.1). It's calmer and more considered but instantly forgettable. The last song of my Bowie odyssey and I'm none the wiser. *"Children round the world put camel shit on the walls. They're making carpets on treadmills or garbage sorting"*. Seems like an apt way to close.

Oh David Bowie you scamp. *Scary Monsters* like so many before offers so much yet remains completely baffling to me. Maybe it's me, maybe my narrow musical mind schooled on hooks and hits can't see or hear what others do. Like a child staring at a Picasso enjoying the pretty colours but unable to see the depth. Then I look at Spotify and the numbers perhaps support my view. Ashes To Ashes 52 million plays , Scary Monsters 14 million, Fashion 12 million, the rest in the low millions (*still millions though Dave*). *Scary Monsters (and Super Creeps)* has some of the highest Bowie highs and a couple of the lowest lows. I really, really wanted to love it but it encapsulates the overriding feeling of this whole exercise in one record. Not the ending I was hoping for but when I come to write an epilogue for this whole project I'll be able to appreciate it for those highs and accept the lows as part of the overall Bowie legend.

Comments from The Afterword

MC Escher says

18/12/2021 at 15:32

You are bang on with your take about the influenced catching up with the ur-influencer. Take another listen to Teenage Wildlife, it's about exactly that (allegedly about Gary Numan in part), but it's also in any decent Bowie top ten song list (okay, maybe top twenty). I love reading all these, Dave. The albums have been part of my musical DNA for 40-plus years so it's really difficult for me to hear them fresh without any preconceptions, and that's what makes these reviews so much fun.

Leffe Gin says

18/12/2021 at 15:48

I've really enjoyed this series. I feel like I've heard this stuff through new ears. I love how honest you are through all of this: you describe what you hear and how you feel, not the usual received wisdom. And yes, Fripp is amazing on this album.

Chiz says

18/12/2021 at 16:12

It was the first Bowie album I was old enough to buy the day it came out. It's No Game 1 is still my favourite album opener. It's astonishing, like nothing I'd ever heard at age 15, and the album just goes on like that, opening one door after another – to funk, atonal guitars, cut-and-jumble lyrics, shouting Japanese ladies... I love it. I suppose I'm biased because this came out just at that moment when I was ready to go beyond chart music and three-minute singles, not that the it doesn't have a couple of those on it. It was the first album I owned that I'd dare to take to school, tucked ostentatiously into the top of my bag so the cool kids might notice it, and 41 years later I think it's still my favourite Bowie album, and his last great one.

Tiggerlion says

18/12/2021 at 17:09

I regard Scary Monsters as a summation of Bowie's seventies. There isn't anything really new, just variations of old magic tricks he'd found rummaging through his bottom drawer. It feels like a conclusion rather than a beginning. For the first time, a Bowie album didn't seem to be coming to us mortals from some point in the future. And you are quite right, Dave, Side One is way better than Two. Kingdom Come and Because You're Young are a struggle, proving conclusively that Pete Townshend does not belong on a Bowie album.

I agree with most of your assessment, however, I love Teenage Wildlife because it's possibly Bowie's first mid-life crisis, brought on by a visit to The Blitz. It's a barbed gift to his successors, the longest track on the album and by no means an easy listen. Fripp actually attempts to reduce its prickliness, softening his "Heroes" solo. Both Roy Bittan who plays piano and Chuck Hammer guitar synthesiser bring an old-fashioned Rock feel. But, mainly, Bowie sounds as if he's having a nervous break-

down. Teenage Wildlife is epic, a stadium filler, a Springsteenesque performance.

The saddest aspect of Scary Monsters for me is the end of George Murray and Dennis Davis, his finest ever rhythm section. The detail they add to Scream Like A Baby, for example, I find spellbinding. Fashion was the last track they recorded. Their march into the distance for the last minute and a half brings a tear to my eye.

I was a regular at The Rum Runner around this time, when Nick Rhodes was the DJ on the Bowie/Roxy nights. I didn't see much leather (too expensive). More make up on the men than the women, though. I sported a faux tartan pair of trousers.

Timbar says

19/12/2021 at 17:53

Well done Dave. I've really enjoyed your run through the albums – and can't wait for your summary! (Can you work out the 3 albums you'd recommend?)

I listened to Scary Monsters a lot when it was released & far preferred it to Lodger. Now, my opinion has completely reversed.

Lodger had an element of "contractual obligation". He discovered that Stage would only count as one album to fulfilling his contract, so the co-writes, changing instruments, and backwards All the Young Dudes, were his way of finding inspiration. Scary Monsters was more polished & commercial, acting as a calling card for his next record deal. Bowie then busied himself with acting & provided RCA with the bare minimum (Baal) while the company released as much material as they could. During the downtime, he studied how the Rolling Stones made all their money from touring & merchandise, before returning, using a known hit producer (Nile Rodgers) allowing him to take charge, produce & arrange the songs, while Bowie made a lot of money.

Locust says

19/12/2021 at 18:42

I'd heard some hits on the radio before, but THE moment when I became aware of Bowie was when the brand new video for Ashes To Ashes was shown on TV, between two regular shows (this was unheard of at the time). It blew me away, the song, the video; I was spellbound. But I didn't buy Scary Monsters as my first Bowie album, I bought the Best Of Bowie vinyl, which was all killer, no filler.

I didn't buy the actual albums until perhaps fifteen years ago (after getting the Platinum Collection on CD first), a few at a time. So I have zero nostalgic feelings towards the albums, but plenty for individual tracks. My personal favourites have become Aladdin Sane and Diamond Dogs, but none of the albums are perfect. While following your Bowie project (very entertaining and interesting!) I've often looked up the album in question and seen that tracks which I can't remember, but your descriptions of makes me want to hear again to see if I agree, are tracks I've deleted from my computer because I didn't like them – definite proof that I have no nostalgic attachment to the albums as artefacts!

I've really enjoyed your reactions, sometimes agreeing, sometimes violently disagreeing, and I hope we'll see more of your writing on the AW, whether a new "series" or stand-alone reviews!

For more comments or to join the conversation go to https://theafterword.co.uk/12-bowie-albums-in-12-months-scary-monsters-and-super-creeps/

Epilogue

Almost a year ago I happened across a tweet from Memorial Device categorically stating that the run of twelve David Bowie albums from *The Man Who Sold The World* to *Scary Monsters* was the greatest run of twelve albums in popular music. At that moment the idea for this project popped into my head and I replied that as I'd never heard a Bowie album before I would listen to one of these albums every month during 2021 and write about it. There seemed to be interest in the idea straight away and some incredulity that I had reached my fifties managing to avoid one. I can understand that; I am a huge advocate for the early eighties being the most adventurous, exciting, imaginative period for pop music so how could I not know Bowie? Well, I know the hits because that's what I'm about but for whatever reason I'd just never bothered. None of my family or peers were Bowie fans so it just never occurred to me. Especially as my real music listening began around 1979 so before that he was just some guy on the radio and a bit of an odd-looking chap off the telly. *Let's Dance* which isn't included here was the album that should have grabbed me but it includes China Girl and I cannot stand China Girl. I'm not a huge fan of the song Let's Dance either to be honest. Makes my decision to impose a twelve month Bowie-a-thon on myself seem even weirder I suppose but I wanted a writing challenge, I wanted to hear something new and I wanted the discipline of stating publicly "I'm going to do this". Also as becomes clear throughout to those who've stuck with it, my Billy Mackenzie obsession and knowing what Bowie meant to him gave me the added impetus to just do it. So I did. Now it's complete this is a summary of my thoughts and the fabulous responses. Also because we all love a list I'll rate them from twelfth down to first. It's clear that everyone will think differently such is the Bowie phenomenon.

My first thought is that this would have been almost impossible without the advent of streaming and specifically for me, Spotify. Had I needed to buy, beg, borrow or steal physical copies of the twelve albums I wouldn't have had a chance. Equally I don't have huge amounts of time to listen to music, so I was really restricted to dog walking and my journey to and from work and it was with Spotify on my phone that I listened. I was determined to give each album a really good go, at least ten listens, probably more. To switch off that part of my brain (no hooks, no chance) that has so defined my music listening over the years and treat each album fairly and with respect. These things obviously mean a lot to a lot of people.

Secondly, and typically for me, I hadn't really thought through how I would frame each review, how would I go about dissecting each one while coming up with something that would interest Bowie fans and those like me that didn't know that much about them. In the end, and again typically for me, I had to wing it. Fortunately, each album presented its own opportunities and very soon I realised my best option was to just say what I heard. Where had Bowie been influenced and how had he influenced others. It proved to be a rich seam allowing me to focus on what I heard and not delving too far into the lyrics, the history, the personalities and the stories behind each album. Millions of words have already been written about them but to my knowledge none have been written from inside my head. Fortunately for me, the real experts and fans here added to each review with their comments without which I would have given up very quickly. So whether it was a straight up review or one of the reimaginings, *Aladdin Sane* as a 70s Top

Of The Pops, *Pin Ups* as a pub rock night out or *Lodger* as a 1979 late night radio show, Bowie gave me something to cling on to. I could not have done this, nor do I believe I could do it again with any other artist. I don't think I could have found such variety, such a wide range of sounds, ideas, imagery and characterisation. It doesn't mean I'm totally sold on the Bowie sound, personally. There's something in his voice that can add so much but equally render some songs almost unlistenable.

I think that hearing them for the first time now rather than when they were released is another huge aspect of this. I've often considered what the impact could have been on me if I'd been 14 or 15 when Ziggy was released or as I said if my brother had brought *"Heroes"* or *Lodger* home instead of *In The City* would my appreciation have been different? I'm sure it would such are the vagaries of where our musical DNA is formed. I feel like it is the one thing I can offer, a completely fresh take drawing on my quite narrow field of reference to show Bowie and his songs in a different light.

Looking back over the reviews I often mention the highs and lows. For the highs I think Life On Mars and "Heroes" have become two of my very favourite songs by anyone and I will absolutely be buying two or three of the albums on vinyl to help tell the story of my small but very personal vinyl collection. As I said very often, without *Station To Station*, *"Heroes"* and *Low* I don't believe there would have been The Associates. This was perhaps my highest high. Being transported back inside the heads of the young Alan Rankine and Billy Mackenzie made this whole project worthwhile on its own. Hearing Bowie's Wild Is The Wind, The Secret Life of Arabia and Boys Keep Swinging after years of just hearing Billy's versions gave them a new life. Discovering new songs like 1984 and Big Brother from *Diamond*

Dogs, the ambient or electronic stuff like Sense of Doubt and Neukölln from *"Heroes"* and Art Decade and Weeping Wall from *Low* was fantastic. Unfortunately, theatrical, screaming trying to be too clever and oblique for his own good, Bowie often left me cold, confused and frustrated and made it almost impossible to love an album as a whole. While his productivity has to be applauded these twelve albums written, recorded, released and toured in 10 years is quite remarkable. For me, however, for what it's worth, occasionally he left out any quality control. I still imagine a single Space-themed album being one of the greatest ever. A full on, all in electronic album being revered in almost biblical terms. Then he could have focused on a theatrical album on a theme that would have run in the West End for years. But what do I know? I still struggle with the concept of someone loving Bowie unconditionally but that's my problem. I will absolutely be looking out for copies of *ChangesOneBowie* and *ChangesTwoBowie*. I've done a playlist choosing two songs from each album that are either my favourites or at least ones that demanded attention. One day I might get around to creating a playlist of the songs I've heard influenced by Bowie.

Overall, despite the lows, one thing is for certain, I absolutely appreciate his talent, his appeal and his sound and vision. I'll defend anyone who is able to write, perform and create a song or album that sells and is appreciated even if it's not to my taste. To deny someone like Bowie would be churlish and ultimately indefensible, he's a complete one off. Whether I'll return often to some of the albums is still open to debate, I think I will because I'd like to hear them without the pressure of wondering what I'm going to write about them. It may bring some freshness I missed the first time round.

I've mentioned the comments already but whether the piano story on *Hunky Dory,* the personal reflections on where you were when you bought an album, heard a song or heard it live, how my writing had made you think or listen again, differences of opinion and even the weird flights of fancy that followed a theme that left Bowie far behind, I have appreciated and loved every one. In many ways I'm a simple man yet scratch the surface I can be quite complicated and I cannot tell you how much all the interaction means to me. Thank you. Meanwhile on Twitter thanks to the continued support from Memorial Device I've had many other engagements including acknowledgements from Pete Paphides and Rusty Egan. Pete said.

"Well, I feel bad that I only finally read your Aladdin Sane review this evening, but also I'm glad I was able to read this one (PinUps) immediately afterwards, as the two reviews made me realise what interesting albums they are in relation to each other – one sounding like an album of covers; while you make a convincing case that the actual covers album coheres better than Aladdin sane. Plus: David Quoie! Superb! Thank you! Xx "

Mind blown.

In final summary, I think David Bowie was a musical genius and he was an even bigger creative genius in the use of imagery to sell that music. Every single cover artwork and characterisation was dramatic and instantly memorable. He was unique and a visionary with an astonishing work ethic and drive to keep creating and changing. He absolutely inspired a generation of artists, some critically acclaimed, some not so, to make music and push the boundaries of what was acceptable. His legacy is not just the music he made but the music he inspired. While I probably remain a hits loving Bowiephile I am now a much more informed one. I can now enter Bowie conversations with some authority and without doubt a whole new appreciation of the man and his place in the history of popular music. Now for that chart which is incredibly difficult because of the variety and inevitable clunkers among the gems on almost every album. I've added a couple of lines from the original review to help explain.

12 / *The Man Who Sold The World*

I can appreciate the invention but sometimes it felt this was in the place of a tune. (Now I sound like my Dad) It felt to me like Bowie was trying to find a style and sound and perhaps didn't believe this was it.

11/ *Young Americans*

It's a nice album that while I can hear all these sounds that I recognise from some of my absolute favourite artists to be honest I wouldn't listen to it again before any of them.

10/ *Scary Monsters and Super Creeps*

Oh David Bowie you scamp. *Scary Monsters* like so many before offers so much yet remains completely baffling to me. Maybe it's me, maybe my narrow musical mind schooled on hooks and hits can't see or hear what others do.

9/ *Aladdin Sane*

It means *Aladdin Sane* is an album of incredible highs and some inexplicable song choices. Bowie was a master at dressing up something familiar in some fancy clothes and make up and selling it as the future.

8/ *The Rise and Fall of Ziggy Stardust and the Spiders From Mars*

So in conclusion I was expecting a concept album full of great songs that matched Bowies latest incarnation. In parts it really is remarkable. In other parts it's just a decent rock album leaning on some Hendrix guitar dressed up in a fancy image.

7/ *Diamond Dogs*

Was he really serious, was he playing up to the arty types and the hipsters while laughing at us and himself? Ultimately what I think matters not a jot and anyway it's just music. I am truly desperate to love Bowie and parts of this album make that happen but then others leave me searching for the skip button.

6/ *Pinups*

It's a brilliant album for me bringing to mind Dr Feelgood, Kilburn and the Highroads, The Blockheads, The Motors and even The Jam on The Who covers. Did Deep Purple ever play a pub? If they did, that's in there too.

5/ *Low*

So there it is. *Low*. It's a grower, it's eclectic, it's Bowie. I have this vision of the recording studio with all these old guitar engineers tripping over wires and extension cables muttering about bloody keyboards while scratching their heads at the noises being called "music".

4/ *Hunky Dory*

Hunky Dory reaches astonishing highs and I'm looking forward to listening to it again away from this over-analysis. There is so much written about Bowie and this album that I don't expect to have found anything especially new. But my view as an outsider looking in might offer a different perspective. This is the album where I think I've started to "get" Bowie.

3/ *Lodger*

One of those albums that from the first listen to the last (probably twenty or so) it was like an explosion of familiar sounds from a time when I was just starting to pay attention to a musical world outside of ABBA and The Wombles.

2/ "Heroes"

So I quite like *"Heroes"* then. I checked the charts for 1977 and it's that period between ABBA and The Sex Pistols in amongst Rod Stewart and The Stranglers and here was Bowie ignoring all that and doing his own thing. Continuing to lay down the template for what was to come when electronic music really exploded.

1/ *Station To Station*

Station To Station will take its place in my collection. A mosquito set in amber from which the DNA of a band and singer that affect me like no other was extracted to create something remarkably similar while remaining thrillingly different.

So there it is. I've changed this a few times while putting the playlist together and I suspect it will change again as I hear some of these albums again but for now that's what I'm putting out there to be judged and dissected. In trying to think of a sign off I've left it to the man himself. This from Big Brother feels just about right to me.

Someone to claim us, someone to follow

Someone to shame us, some brave Apollo

Someone to fool us, someone like you

www.ingramcontent.com/pod-product-compliance
Ingram Content Group UK Ltd.
Pitfield, Milton Keynes, MK11 3LW, UK
UKHW020240250726
13967UKWH00001B/477